# STEADY YOUR

# *Spooky Horse*

### How-To Methods
#### from the
### Mounted Police

by Jim Barrett

## The Russell Meerdink Company, Ltd.
## Neenah, Wisconsin 54956 U.S.A.

Cover design & layout by Bosetti Production Art & Design

**Library of Congress Cataloging-in-Publication Data**

Barrett, Jim, 1948-
    Steady your spooky horse : how-to methods from the mounted police / by Jim Barrett.
        p. cm.
    ISBN-13: 978-0-929346-79-3 (hardcover)
    1. Police horses. 2. Horses--Training. 3. Horses--Psychology. I. Title.

    HV7957.B37 2005
    363.2'32--dc22

                    2005010749

Published by

**The Russell Meerdink Company, Ltd.**
1555 South Park Avenue, Neenah, Wisconsin 54956
USA
(920) 725-0955
www.horseinfo.com

Printed in the United States of America

# TABLE OF CONTENTS

# DISCLAIMER

The techniques and methods contained in this book are drawn from the author's many years of experience and knowledge in this field. However, this book is not intended to be all-inclusive on the subject matter and may not apply in all situations.While this book does contain some training information, the reader should consult with and obtain a professional trainer or experienced horse person before applying these techniques on a particular horse or in a specific circumstance. Neither the author nor the publisher assume any liability or make any guarantees of any nature for any outcome resulting from the use of techniques contained in this book.

## REMEMBER - RIDING A HORSE
## IS A HAZARDOUS ACTIVITY

# ACKNOWLEDGEMENT

There are a number of people that I must thank for making this book possible. First and foremost my wife Judy who has stood by me through many years of toiling in this very challenging aspect of the horse world. Judy also acts as the first level of quality control because she invariably edits the rough drafts. Without her continuing support, this work would not have been possible.

I have had the opportunity to train under two of the premier horse trainers/instructors in the United States. Clyde Kennedy, a former Los Angeles Police Department Mounted trainer, was my first exposure to an individual who not only truly understood horses, but also believed in their ability to accomplish a policing mission.

Richard Shrake has helped me tremendously in the evolution of the ideas that are presented in this book. Through Richard's certification process, I have learned the meaning of Resistance Free™ Training. I have grown as a horseman under Richard's tutelage and I thank him for sharing his knowledge.

Kris Seals, who essentially wrote Chapter 4 of this book, has been a huge influence in my life. Kris is a premier West Coast police dressage instructor who has helped many officers connect with their mounts. Kris is not only good in the arena, but also capable of putting her actions into words.

Wendall Hildebrandt and Elmo Sheeran who have both spent a life-time around horses, and especially police horses, have leant a lot of their knowledge contained in these pages. Ditto for Kirk Smith of the

Los Angeles Police Department who has a firm grasp on life-saving tactical considerations for mounted officers. Stan Buscovich, who recently retired from the San Francisco Police Department, has also been an influence. He is recognized as an expert in the field of police color guards and mounted ceremonial protocol.

Dr. Robert Miller, through conversations and his book entitled Understanding the Ancient Secrets of the Horse's Mind, has helped me to focus my thoughts on sensory training. I reference his book in this work because Dr. Miller has clearly explained what many of us always knew but did not put into words.

Patricia Fry who has been my mentor while I authored both A Manual for the Mounted Officer and this work. Patty has patiently educated me about the publishing business and even consented to do the copy editing on this work.

There are literally hundreds of other people, both police officers and non-cops who, through some interaction, have helped to shape this book. For all of those folks, a big "thank you" for sharing your knowledge.

Finally, this book is an attempt to present ideas that will help people to be safer when they are enjoying a relationship with their equine friend. If that is accomplished then the effort involved in writing this book has been well worth it!

Jim Barrett
Ojai, California

# Foreword

When I graduated from veterinary school in 1956 the horse population of the United States was down to slightly over two million, one tenth of what it had been half a century earlier. The working horse was on its way out, replaced by modern mechanical devices. Today, half a century later, the horse population is on its way back up. Now, at about seven million, the increase is almost entirely in horses used for recreational purposes. Even on cattle ranches, horse numbers are down, the required number reduced by the increasing use of ATVs, pickup trucks, and helicopters.

An exception to this diminished need for working horses is in law enforcement. Horses are required to patrol our borders, parks, wilderness areas, and for search and rescue operations. But, it is for urban police work that the horse has proven invaluable.

This became known to me one evening in the '60s. I was attending a national veterinary convention in New York City and had been invited to dinner in Greenwich Village. It was a warm spring evening and still daylight. At a major intersection, well over a thousand "street people" had gathered. They loafed, chattered and shared drugs; most of them attired in the "hippy" garb typical of that era.

We stopped to view the unfamiliar scene when we saw three mounted NYPD officers quietly riding down one of the streets. Remember that these were the days when the approach of several police cars would have provoked shouts of "pig!," and a storm of beer bottles and cans.

As the officers neared the intersection they quietly turned their tall, calm horses, whose necks and heads were elegantly flexed, sideways. Then they side passed into the intersection, essentially blocking the width of the street they were on.

The Sergeant spoke softly and kindly, "Ok folks, let's move along now. Let's not block traffic. Move along please."

The crowd melted away quietly before the horses, and eventually dispersed.

At one point a young woman, typically clothed in an ankle length dress, with bare feet, and long hair encircled with a halo of flowers, ran out of the crowd towards the mounted officers. I thought she was going to spit upon the Sergeant, but instead, she stopped, petted the horse's nose, kissed it, and ran back into the crowd.

That's when I first realized the value of using horses to control urban crowds.

Some time later I took a taxicab to an appointment. Two blocks from my destination we got stuck in a traffic gridlock. Hundreds of cars were immobilized and every driver held the horn button down, producing a cacophony of sound. I decided to walk the remaining distance to my destination and paid the driver.

As I threaded my way through the cars and trucks, deafened by the noise, here came a NYPD mounted officer. His horse calmly and efficiently worked his way through the maze and finally after reaching a key point, the officer directed traffic and unsnarled the gridlock.

Again, I was awed by how effective horses can be in urban police work, and especially impressed by how superbly trained both the horse and its rider were.

Not long afterwards an unfortunate incident occurred in Yosemite National Park at a hippy encampment. Illegal drugs were being used blatantly. A group of park personnel, mounted on horses, charged the mob, hooting and swinging lariat ropes. The unruly crowd pulled the officers off their horses and beat them severely. When I read about this incident, the importance of proper training for both the officers and the horses became very evident.

This book, although inspired by the author's experience as a mounted police officer, is important for every rider and every horse owner. Ideally, every domesticated horse should be "bombproof." That is an attainable goal; one which the chapters which follow will facilitate.

Robert Miller, DVM

Thousand Oaks, California

To Judy

# Preface

This book is a "spin off" from *A Manual for the Mounted Officer*, published in September of 2002. After writing the manual it became obvious to me, mainly through bombproofing seminars that I was conducting for civilian groups, that there is a need for a reference explaining sensory training to the general public. Out of that realization, this book moved from concept to reality.

The need to be safer while riding a horse is not a new notion. The very first time someone fell off of a horse thousands of years ago, that realization was probably born. It no doubt hurt then just as it does today. While the concern is not new, the theory that intense sensory training can prevent accidents is relatively recent. We now know that a person can "bombproof" or "spookproof" a horse.

This important concept is a by-product of police horse training and an overall understanding by horse people that they want to be safer no matter what their daily equine activities. In fact, horse people are just reflecting the trend emphasizing personal safety that is part of American culture today. As an example, 25 years ago the auto industry had a very difficult time selling safety items in their cars. People were not interested in paying extra for added protection. Today that has changed dramatically as consumers actively seek out safety equipment when considering the purchase of a new vehicle. This philosophy has spilled over into the horse world as well.

Increased numbers of police mounted units, driven by philosophies of community-oriented policing in which the public is free to interact with law enforcement, has planted this seed of change in the horse industry. In addition, volunteerism in the police service, especially volunteer mounted units, has increased tremendously in the last 10 years. Thus, many more horse owners are directly involved in some type of Sheriff or Police Posse, Mounted Search and Rescue or Ranger group. Most civilian volunteers must pass some type of testing process in order to qualify their mounts. In most jurisdictions, preparation for a qualification process for horse and rider is often rooted in varying degrees in sensory training.

Even horse owners who are not directly involved with law enforcement are intrigued with the ability of a police officer to sit on a horse in the middle of a busy intersection or perhaps under a Ferris wheel. This simple act goes against most people's preconceived notions of what a horse is all about. When horse owners see this they immediately think, "Well, my horse would never do that!" or perhaps, "How can I get my mount to stand quietly in similar circumstances?" This book is an attempt to answer that question through the presentation of a system for desensitizing your horse.

While I talk about systems in the body of this work, it is important to realize that the Horse Sensory Training System (HSTS)™ includes components of daily riding. Some people think that spookproofing a horse should take an afternoon. This is absolutely NOT THE CASE! Truly desensitizing a horse is similar to any other horse training; it takes hours and hours in order to get to the level that is satisfactory. What the reader will find in this book is a way to accomplish this training. But like all horse training, it should be accomplished systematically over time. This fundamental concept cannot be overstated!

For the average horse owner, the most challenging portion of the HSTS™ is contained in Chapter 7 where the concept of Stimulus Training is explored. Stimulus training is known by a number of different names, including nuisance training, habituation training or hazing training. Whatever it is called, it is an effort to desensitize the horse through the introduction of sensory stimuli that are not normally encountered on a typical day of riding. The concept is to encourage the equine to face and defeat its innate fear of the unknown object through successful repetition of "facing and overcoming." When stimulus training is competently done, it works, as is proven by the many thousands of police horses that successfully work the streets throughout the world.

Some trainers think that desensitizing a horse is the same as de-energizing the animal. This is not the case. Police horses can excel at a number of non-police related events – even speed events – and still work well on the streets. Desensitizing a horse is more about understanding an individual horse's energy level and learning to use and control that energy, rather than attempting to eliminate it. This is accomplished through the application of the HSTS™ that is discussed in this book.

# CHAPTER 1

# Understanding the Psychology of Your Horse

One of the most important aspects of horse ownership is to truly understand what makes this complex animal tick. The horse, as a large, living, breathing and thinking creature has the opportunity to significantly impact the lives of individuals with whom it comes in contact. A failure to recognize and understand certain behavior can mean that the significant impact is all negative. Avoiding the negative and accentuating the positive is highly desirable in horse ownership, because, quite frankly, it can mean the difference between a pleasurable day with your horse or a trip to the hospital. To avoid that ambulance ride, there are nine key understandings to explore.

## KEY UNDERSTANDING #1

Horses think like horses, period! No matter how compelled we, as humans, are to imbue our thought processes onto the horse, this animal will never reason or use human logic to make decisions. The horse can use only those tools that Mother Nature has provided over the million years of its existence. Therefore, in order to be successful with his thought process, we must enter the horse's world because it cannot enter ours.

# KEY UNDERSTANDING #2

Horses are first and foremost a herd animal. Their comfort, in fact their very existence, revolves around the herd and their individual relationship within that herd. Even if the horse you own has never been outside of a box stall, it is still a herd animal. Equine instincts are so ingrained in each individual that they cannot be erased even if the horse has not "run wild" with its brethren. Because horses are herd animals, space domination within and among the herd can mean the difference between life and death for any individual. In the wild, the survival of an individual may depend on which other horses dominate and control its movement.[1] Therefore a horse that is at the bottom of the pecking order may eat and drink last, causing it to  be a weaker animal and more subject to sudden death from predators. Horses have a fundamental understanding of this dynamic that cannot be erased from their memory banks.

The herd is a very structured society with leaders (generals), mid-managers (majors, captains) and privates, who are dominated by all others in the hierarchy.[2] The entire herd looks to the generals to provide the leadership and to perform the most important of jobs – keeping all the members safe. When the human enters the horse's herd, the horse quickly categorizes him as to his place in the hierarchy. The horse's understanding, or the human's misunderstanding, of this basic group dynamic may forever shape the relationship of the human and the equine.

# KEY UNDERSTANDING #3

Horses speak body language.[3] They are constantly sending out cues to others, and that includes humans. This body language is spatial in nature because horses seldom speak to each other from a distance. Instead, they send non-verbal cues as they interact in the herd. A private clearly understands the major's pinned ears or swinging rear-end when the private is within kicking range. However, from a distance this horse will not necessarily acknowledge or react to the non-verbal cues of a more dominant animal. That is because it realizes that there is nothing to fear from an instantaneous reaction (i.e. the kick).

The equine's use of its eye is also a form of communication. Horses avoid direct eye contact with others. The horse instinctively understands that predatory animals greatly rely on the use of their eyes in hunting during which they do make direct eye contact, especially at the time of the kill. Conversely, the softening of the eye is tantamount to the opposite of direct eye contact. A horse willing to give to the more dominant member of the herd, even if that is a human, will soften its eye in submission.

Finally, every human contact with a horse is a training session. Good or bad, when the human interacts with the horse, training is happening. Because I strongly believe this I use owner, rider and trainer interchangeably throughout this book.

## KEY UNDERSTANDING #4

Horses are extremely sensitive to stimuli that humans may not even notice.[4] Their sense of smell, hearing, touch, taste and sight have been highly refined over the years because without them, the horse would not have survived. As an example, the equine, which is a surefooted animal, is keenly aware of surfaces that it walks upon. A horse knows instantly from the feel (touch) when it is stepping upon a surface with which it is unfamiliar. That knowledge may cause the horse to balk in order to avoid the unknown.

## KEY UNDERSTANDING #5

Along with its keen senses, go the horse's incredibly quick reactions. Just throw your hand up in its face and see how quickly the horse moves its head. This reaction time has also been fundamental to its survival. Physiologically the horse can instantaneously turn a decision into an action. This quickness is often deceiving because the horse is such a large animal.[5] But anyone who has had a horse spook and "swap ends" can testify to the speed of its movement and the resultant hardness of the ground.

## KEY UNDERSTANDING #6

Horses have survived over the eons by running away. You do not have to go to a horse race to understand that, anatomically, the horse is built to run.[6] In the wild, the horse occupied the grasslands of the continents. This habitat was conducive to running, thus to survival. A key understanding about the horse is that when the chips are down, the first instinct is to rapidly depart the area.

## KEY UNDERSTANDING #7

Horses must learn very quickly. Slow learners are eliminated from the herd by predatory animals.[7] There is little room for error or misjudgment in the wild of the plains.

## KEY UNDERSTANDING #8

Horses never forget, but fortunately for humans, they do forgive.[8] They categorize all learned experiences in three compartments. 1. There are things in the world to be feared and therefore to flee. 2. There are things to note and deal with in some manner other than flight (i.e. sniffing, spinning, backing, or some other reaction) and 3. Some things just need to be accepted and/or ignored. Horses' excellent memory is ultimately why they are so trainable. Once they realize through training and continuous exposure or desensitization that just about any item can be tolerated, they eventually reach number three above, which makes for a very well trained animal.

## KEY UNDERSTANDING #9

Horses are quickly desensitized to stimuli. If this was not so, the horse would be constantly running away from the next scary thing and would not have time to do those other basics of life such as eating, drinking, resting, procreating, etc.[9] In nature, they soon learn to ignore or at least accept the blowing tumble-weed, electrical storm and other common hazards of the plains. It is this ability to accept stimulus that is one of the keys to mankind's success in desensitizing the equine.

## KEY UNDERSTANDING #10

Horses, like humans, learn at different rates. While there is no known I.Q. test for horses, it is obvious that some are more intelligent than others. Trainers must understand learning rates when doing sensory training because the added stress can have a great impact on a horse's ability to learn. In fact, when a horse is over-stressed its fragile psyche can, in essence, "shut down" and little to no learning occurs.

Each of these key understandings plays a critical part in fully comprehending the psychological makeup of the horse. However, it is through using all of the key understandings that man has been successful in training and using the horse to his benefit. As an example, if an owner does not understand the significance of the horse's memory in the training process, he may actually de-train an animal by injuring it. In effect, the trainer has dropped a black marble in the horse's brain that may never be erased.[10] The horse will remember this experience for its lifetime and may always react a certain way when placed in a circumstance similar to that when it was injured.

These key understandings are cornerstones in the continuous process of sensory training or bombproofing the horse. The desensitizing system contained in this book is a continuation of a process that started on the day the horse was born. Someone petted the newborn for the first time. Someone haltered that animal and eventually led it somewhere. As time passed, the horse was desensitized to the feel of the saddle, then weight in the saddle and a method of control (bit) in its mouth. All of these occurrences were desensitization processes that built upon each other, the results of which now make up the equine package that you climb upon from day to day. However, that does not mean that this process should ever stop. In fact, having a truly bombproof horse is a lifelong endeavor for both horse and rider.

It is critical for all horse owners to be thoroughly familiar with each of the key understandings. Failing to understand them may result in a trainer or rider not making the necessary adjustments to accommodate the horse's reactions in the training regimen. As an example, in order to successfully desensitize the equine, the trainer must be the dominant member of the relationship. If that does not occur, the horse will be making the decisions for the herd, albeit just a herd of two, and this is a mathematical formula for disaster. In order to ensure domination, the trainer must learn the language of the horse and "speak" to the animal so he will understand. This does not mean bigger whips and sharper spurs, but rather domination through positional and spatial control.

# First Lesson Learned

I first realized how important it is to use the Horse Sensory Training System (though we did not have a name for it then) in the early '80s when I attended a large police department's mounted academy. What a disaster! I arrived at the training site with a horse that I had owned for about a week. This horse, who I called Tattoo because of his many brands, was a big, stout and very athletic gray quarter horse. Basically, I showed up with Tattoo and he showed up with an attitude.

It soon became apparent that I was in way over my head. I knew nothing about this horse and he definitely did not trust me. The training was very intense, running easily into 10-hour days, with a half-hour fireworks display as the grand finale each night. By day four, what little we had as a relationship had deteriorated. I was convinced that Tattoo was out to kill me and he confirmed my worst fears by launching me into a cement culvert. Obviously, his frustration level had piqued so he sent me an unmistakable message. In spite of his statement, I climbed back up and we were able to complete the day.

One of the trainers, a well-known horseman in Southern California, saved my bacon. His advice made it possible for Tattoo and me to finish the school. Tattoo turned out to be a great police horse and he and I were partners for over 10 years.

But I learned a valuable lesson. The bond of trust between horse and rider must be well established before even considering training of this nature.

# Bibliographic Notes

[1] Robert M. Miller, *Understanding the Ancient Secrets of the Horse's Mind*, The Russell Meerdink Company Ltd., 1999, p. 17.

[2] Richard Shrake, *Resistance Free Training*, Trafalgar Square Publishing, 2000, p. 13.

[3] Robert M. Miller, *Understanding the Ancient Secrets of the Horse's Mind*, The Russell Meerdink Company Ltd., 1999, p. 53.

[4] Robert M. Miller, *Understanding the Ancient Secrets of the Horse's Mind*, The Russell Meerdink Company Ltd., 1999, p. 23.

[5] Robert M. Miller, *Understanding the Ancient Secrets of the Horse's Mind*, The Russell Meerdink Company Ltd., 1999, p. 15.

[6] Ibid.

[7] Robert M. Miller, *Understanding the Ancient Secrets of the Horse's Mind*, The Russell Meerdink Company Ltd., 1999, p. 16.

[8] Ibid.

[9] Ibid.

[10] Richard Shrake, *Resistance Free Training*, Trafalgar Square Publishing, 2000, p. 24.

# CHAPTER 2

# Selecting That Perfect Horse

One of the most significant and difficult things any horse owner will do is select and buy a horse. Whether you are a first time buyer or have had years of experience, purchasing a horse can put sweat on your brow. Most horse owners do not raise horses and therefore buy them with a minimal knowledge of how the horse was raised and trained. Indeed, the horse you are considering may have had several owners before being offered to you. This can be a problem, especially for the novice horse purchaser who must make a decision based on the health, conformation, training and personality of a horse in a brief period of inspection. And let's face it, there are plenty of unscrupulous "horse swappers" who will take advantage of novices and experienced people alike.

While there are a number of good publications available that cover how to buy a horse, few of them discuss selecting a horse with the physical attributes and personality that is conducive to sensory training. Ultimately, purchasing a good sensible horse – and therefore one that will be quick to accept sensory training – has the potential to provide the owner years of positive experiences. Finding that animal is the challenge.

It is readily apparent that one cannot even ride a horse that is unsound because of one or more of the many equine maladies. Therefore, a decision about veterinarian exams is often the first hurdle to face. There are several schools of thought about the value of pre-sale vet checks. Many people who purchase horses set a dollar limit for the vet check since they can become very expensive, especially if blood tests and x-rays are taken. Other purchasers have vet checks on horses based on the value of the horse (i.e. the higher value, the more likely a vet check will be done). The decision to have a pre-sale veterinary check is up to the purchaser and is often based upon the purchaser's comfort factor. However, a minimal vet check can save the potential horse owner from purchasing a horse that is physically incapable of performing the work the buyer intends to do.

Modern day riding, especially if it is done on hard surfaces such as asphalt and pavement, can take its toll on any horse, so you certainly do not want to start out purchasing a horse with undetected leg or foot problems. This is where the decision to x-ray becomes important. While many vets are adept at spotting lameness, especially after flex tests are done, others are not. Today more and more vets who do pre-sale checks find the need to x-ray not only the feet and knee joints, but also the hocks and the fetlocks. While this precautionary exercise may help you to avoid a very expensive problem down the road, it must be balanced with the cost of taking all of those x-rays.

Pre-sale horses should have their feet tested for navicular syndrome, contracted heels or abscesses. All of these can cause a considerable amount of down time for the horse. In the case of navicular syndrome, it can put the horse out of commission permanently. Horses that require special shoeing no matter what the cause should be avoided.

In order to successfully sensory train your horse, he must have good eyesight both day and night (no night blindness). Horses that do not see well are often surprised by the world as it suddenly comes into focus. Therefore, special emphasis should be placed on the health of the eyes.

The need for solid conformation cannot be stressed enough. Horses that are well-built have fewer physical problems. Horses that are constantly sore because of leg, back, neck or foot problems are generally less accepting of the world. That makes them harder to train for anything, especially sensory training. Remember that the vet check should be the last step, after the horse is determined to be satisfactory in all other ways.

In the world of horse purchasing, the "two heads are better than one" rule definitely applies. Take a knowledgeable friend or professional trainer along to help evaluate the horse. They may see something that you overlook which could make the difference as to whether you truly want to write that check. Additionally, a friend can better observe the budding relationship between you and the horse.

Follow the conformation and health checks with tests to ensure the horse's personality can withstand sensory training. Sensory tests are shown on the following pages.

## Determining the Fear Factor

There are a number of tests that can be done to help determine the "fear factor" of a horse. One of the most common is to "sack out" a horse with a bright white towel. With the horse on a lead rope, slowly present the towel. Shake it in front of the horse's head, rub it on the horse's back and sides, and loop it over the

Santa Ynez Horse Trainer Christina Barnes introduces a white towel to Skippy, a 5-year-old horse owned by Ken Olgle. He is definitely taking a look.

Christina moves the towel around the horse's head.
Skippy is very tolerant of this stimuli.

When the handler moves the towel to the horse's back, it becomes a little more concerned as you can see by the raised head and ear movement.

horse's neck. You may also try wrapping the towel around the horse's head or swatting the horse under the barrel. Each of these may or may not elicit some type of reaction. Of course, judging the reaction is the key to this test. If the horse shies dramatically, backs quickly, spins or attempts to leave the area, then it is probably going to present some challenges during sensory training. However, if the horse is attempting to avoid the towel without dramatic movement, it may be useful with further training. And finally, if the horse stands quietly while you "haze" it with the towel, then it is certainly worthy of future consideration.

You may also consider a horse that is younger

With a little work, Skippy obviously has no problem with the towel.

and has not had a lot of experience with sensory items if it displays curiosity during the "towel test." If the untied horse backs up when approached from the front, but stands after the pressure is relieved and then stretches to smell what is in your hand, you can bet it is trainable to sensory items. If a horse turns away from the towel, but its curiosity causes it to turn back, then this horse has some potential for training. I score horses high if they are willing to face their fears, no matter what their age. They get even higher scores if they will take a step or two toward that scary towel during the testing process and are obviously thinking about how to deal with the item without running away.

If the animal you are considering passes the "towel test," then move on to an item that adds noise to the formula. A gunnysack filled with aluminum cans or a plastic container partially filled with pebbles will fit the bill. Again, while holding the horse in hand intro-duce the item slowly by lightly shaking it. Continue this process, until the animal begins to accept the item or shows you, unequivocally, that it does not intend to tolerate this stimulus. If the horse is accepting, increase the noise level at a consistent rate on both sides of its body near the head. Do not proceed past his shoulder with the noisy item. This could result in your being "cow kicked."

Many horses are overly concerned about the surfaces that they walk upon. In order to get an idea about a horse's future ability to tolerate a variety of surfaces, test it over something wooden. Many ranches have portable wooden bridges, but absent that, a piece of plywood can be placed on the ground to test the horse. When first doing this, take the horse in hand and lead it across the bridge. Do not stand directly in front of a horse while attempting to lead the animal across an obstacle. Horses will often jump an item rather then step on it and you definitely do not want to be in the landing zone.

If the horse readily walks over the bridge, add an additional challenge by placing a canvas or plastic tarp on the ground. However, if the horse did not walk over the wooden bridge, the chances of getting it over plastic are very slim. If the horse is young and would not walk over the wooden or plastic surfaces, but shows a great deal of curiosity, there is hope that, with further training, the horse will tolerate the stimulus. Once you have been successful in getting the horse to lead over a wooden bridge (also see Chapter 7) then give it a try while riding. Again, be aware that the horse may find the need to leap the bridge rather than walk upon it even if it has performed well in hand.

It is a good idea to work a horse over a wooden object or bridge. This horse is standing quietly on the wooden platform.

If the horse has done a good job with the testing thus far, then it is time to see its reaction to traffic or common street scenes before writing the check. Prior to riding any horse or taking one near city streets, thoroughly interview the person who regularly rides the horse. This may not be the seller. At a minimum, find out if the horse is normally ridden near traffic. Has this horse ever been in a parade, has it ever had any type of sensory training (probably not) and what are its normal reactions under stress? These are important questions, and the answers may change your mind about this particular horse. Be wary of the seller who avoids answering your questions. If the seller is apprehensive about you riding near the street, you should take a pass on doing so (and probably pass on the horse as well).

I like to ride the horse to a location near a street that is fairly busy. However, during the testing process I will not take a horse onto the street (nor do I recommend that you do so), because there are too many uncontrollable variables and I know little about the animal I am riding. A dirt field or orchard that is adjacent to a busy street is my choice. The horse is getting some exposure to traffic and you are gaining important information without actually walking on asphalt or risking the chance of the horse being "over-exposed" to sensory stimuli.

Even riding next to a busy street can expose a horse to moving vehicles, loose dogs, kids on bikes, parents with baby carriages, children jumping on skateboards, or just about anything else imaginable. What is critical in this process is your evaluation of the horse's reactions. Did he "cruise" along, looking but not reacting? Or did the horse jump at every blowing piece of paper and car that went by? Or was it somewhere in between – reacting to some things but ignoring others? At this stage it is important to objectively evaluate the horse's reactions. Do not let your emotions and an innate admiration for horses fog your perception of an individual horse's ability to accept the testing you are conducting.

This is also a good time to get input from a knowledgeable friend or trainer. The additional pair of eyes can be extremely helpful in evaluating the horse's reactions. And remember, when riding a horse that you know little about, always wear your helmet!

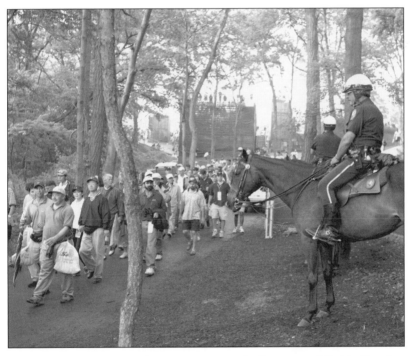

Nassau County (NY) Police Department mounted officers control foot traffic after an event. A calm, steady demeanor is essential for police horses and for any horse you plan to stimulus train.

Courtesy Kevin Kane, Nassau County Police Department.

# Trainability

Because we are asking the horse to do something foreign to it, it is critical that the horse we select be trainable. Again, this can be very difficult to determine in the short period of time you may be testing the horse prior to a purchase.

Trainability is closely connected to the overall attitude of the horse. Many horses enjoy learning new things and will give 100 percent for their riders.

Others do not want to be bothered. One simple test to determine the horse's attitude (and therefore, trainability) is to disengage its hip. This is easily accomplished by taking the unsaddled horse in hand with a lead rope and moving it away from you while you are standing at its hip. Slight forward pressure is put on the rope to get the horse's feet moving forward, while the horse is forced to step through its mid-line with the rear foot closest to you. As you step toward the hip, the horse should move away from your body quietly, with a minimum of resistance or tugging on the lead rope. When doing this do not forget to repeat this maneuver on both sides of the horse. The horse should be respectful of your body position. It should move when your feet move, and not be "wringing" its tail or pinning its ears. If the horse does either of those things, it is probably telling you that future training is going to come at a cost.

Initially, you may have to use your hand on the horse's side to get it to move away from you. However, if you must continually poke the horse in the side, or worry it with your hand or rope to get it to move, this

Christina is disengaging the horse's hip by asking for forward movement with her right hand and stepping into his space with her body. Notice that she is moving her feet in time with the movement of Skippy's hind legs.

Remember to disengage the horse's hip from both sides.

horse is probably going to be resistant to training. Conversely, if it takes off and runs around you while you are holding the lead rope, this horse may very well be overly sensitive on its sides or lack the maturity to accomplish the upcoming training.

This test also gives you a chance to take a psychological snapshot of the horse's mind. Is this animal a General and insisting that you prove to it that it must move? Or is it a Private and very willing to give into your efforts to dominate? These are important questions and you should know the answers before making a purchase.

Another simple test is to rub your thumb or knuckles along both sides of the horse's rib cage from about the cinch to the hip. Apply a moderate amount of pressure and watch for the reaction of the horse. If it stands quietly, or perhaps cocks its head to determine what you are doing, the horse is being very accepting of this aggravation. If the horse swishes its tail or moves sideways to avoid your thumb, this horse may present some difficulties during training. If it swings its head to bite or tries to cow-kick, then pass on this prospect.

Christina is doing the "thumb test" on Skippy. Notice that it is certainly paying attention and gave her a slight "swish" of the tail, but was generally very tolerant of this test.

Another thing to look for prior to making a purchase is head tossing. Besides being dangerous for horse and rider alike, this is definitely a key to a horse's attitude. A horse may use head tossing as an avoidance tactic. It is the animal's way of refusing the rider's instructions. If there is no medical or dental reason that can be fixed, let someone else deal with this problem because it can be difficult to remedy.

All horses must walk willingly into horse trailers and ride quietly. Fortunately, the slant load trailers have eliminated a lot of problems that used to be inherent in transporting horses. However, there are still a number of horses that have had bad experiences with trailers and can become balky upon entry or scramble while being transported. Transportation issues can be difficult to fix. It is recommended that horses with trailering problems be avoided.

## What Does Age Have To Do With It?

In a word, everything. Generally older horses are simply more tolerant of new and unexpected experiences than young animals. This can be critically important when it comes to bombproofing unless you find that rare youngster who has the mind of a 20-year-old. When you are attempting to sensory train that three-year-old, patience, patience and more patience will be needed. In fact, you may find yourself putting this process on hold until a later date, essentially waiting for maturity to help.

Having said that, it has been noted that very young horses, less than three months old, are often very tolerant of sensory training. Horses at this age, especially if they have been imprint trained at birth, accept items that they would not tolerate at age three. Additionally, the human is able to "muscle" the very young horse through some of the more frightening obstacles, which you cannot do when they are three-year-olds.

The ideal age for successful sensory training is generally between 8 and 14 years. Older horses are easier, but there are so many potential medical issues that you must balance the ease of training with the number of anticipated riding years.

## Breed

Does breed matter? The answer is yes. While there are individual horses of any breed that can be completely bombproofed, some breeds are easier than others. In fact, many mixed breed horses – "Heinz 57," parentage unknown – are the easiest to get through sensory training and often have the added attraction of being less expensive to purchase. The "hot breeds" such as Arabians and Thoroughbreds can present real challenges. But do not fault the horse. They were bred for purposes not necessarily conducive to sensory training.

## Ideal Selection Process

The ideal selection process is to test your prospective horse for a 30-day period before making a purchase. Many police departments have this criteria written into their policy and procedures. While this allows the agency or an individual to get a good, long look at the animal, it may be difficult for the seller to accommodate. The seller may have fiscal considerations, or quite frankly, may not want the buyer to know too much about the animal. Additionally, there are issues about who is responsible if the horse is injured during the 30-day period. As long as the responsibility for the horse is clearly delineated in writing and the seller is agreeable, a 30-day test period is the ideal way to go.

# Second Lesson Learned

I learned a second lesson at that large police department's mounted academy that I attended in the early '80s. That lesson is that 8-10 hours of sensory training is too much for the average horse, even a very calm animal. Sensory training needs to be taken in manageable amounts and interspersed with other equine activities.

Therefore, in a typical sensory training day, two to three hours of exposure to "scary items" is a long time. Not only do horses display symptoms of burn out if it goes longer, but the riders also become irritated with the training. After all, psychologically both horses and humans can withstand only so much stress!

Sessions of ground work, equitation training, or trail riding actually promote success during a day of difficult sensory training.

I recall on day four of the mounted academy that the staff informed us that we were going on a trail ride. Since Tattoo and I were both suffering from sensory overload, I thought, "What great news!" That was until I found out that this outfit's version of a trail ride was considerably different than mine.

Instead of enjoying the manicured riding trails of a nearby park, we ended up on one of the city's busiest streets, dodging buses and garbage trucks. It was while returning from this ride that Tattoo informed me that he had had enough by unloading me.

However, I am grateful for the experience because I learned an important lesson. Time management is critical to success and the sensory training should be done in bite-sized amounts!

# CHAPTER 3

# A Systems Approach
# to Sensory Training

It takes a systems approach to bombproof your horse. What is a system? It is something we, as humans, use daily. As an example, you have a system for loading the dishwasher, a system for mowing the lawn, a system for washing the car and there is even a system for writing a book. Let us look at a system for loading a dishwasher.

After removing the dishes from the table (the first part of the system), you pre-wash them by rinsing the large food particles off of each plate. You then open the washer door, pull out the appropriate rack for plates and begin to put them into the washer, usually loading from one side to the other. You continue this system until the dishes are all loaded, you have placed soap in the appropriate slot, closed the dishwasher door and turned it on.

It is highly likely that the system you employ is nearly the same every time you do it. It's probably highly effective as it creates both physical and psychological comfort. In other words, that's the way you like to do it. As humans we generally work well within parameters of any system that we employ to accomplish a task.

A system, then, is made up of individual components or actions that are used in combination in order to accomplish the task at hand. These individual components are not unique to just one person. As an example, if you watched 10 people load a dishwasher, you would find that most of them accomplish this task by using very similar individual actions. Ultimately, it is the combination of the actions, in a specific order, that makes up the system employed to load a dishwasher. In essence, a system can be employed for a task as simple as loading a dishwasher or mowing the lawn to one as complicated as putting a man on the moon. No matter what the project, consistency in the order and application of the actions is what ultimately produces the workable system and thus success.

## THE HORSE SENSORY
## TRAINING SYSTEM (HSTS)™

How does a system relate to bombproofing your equine partner? The answer is best illustrated by what you do not do in order to accomplish this task. You do not get up one Saturday morning, gather up a large red ball (that your horse has never seen before), ask your spouse to hold ole Buttercup and start tossing the ball at the horse. This is an example of an unsystematic approach to the process. And since horses like to operate on many of the same psychological planes as humans (they especially appreciate predictable actions), ole Buttercup may very well dislocate your partner's shoulder in its haste to quit the field.

In order to avoid this scenario I advocate the use of the Horse Sensory Training System (HSTS)™ which is a ground-up approach to bombproofing your horse. HSTS™ is comprised of several easy-to-understand "hallmarks" for horse and handler to complete. After reaching each hallmark, the pair is then ready to move to the next step. The end result is a horse that will be as sensible and quiet as possible.

Starting on the ground with horse in hand is the beginning of building a relationship between two individuals, one horse and one human, that will result in a team. You'll progress to riding the horse in a controlled environment while you learn to push the correct buttons and help the horse to accept the relationship. The next step is to ride outside the controlled environment allowing the horse more freedom of movement. This will further strengthen the relationship. You will eventually get to the point where you can introduce the horse to various sensory situations which it can tolerate because the team of human and horse has begun to gain confidence in each other.

## TABLE OF HALLMARKS

How do you know when you are working systematically to accomplish a hallmark? This table will assist you in understanding these important accomplishments.

| ACTION | HALLMARK REACHED |
|---|---|
| Reading and understanding the key understandings | Truly comprehending what makes horses tick |
| Standing in front of the horse's shoulder | Rider "squares up" and consistently stands in front of the shoulder while facing the horse |
| Disengaging the horse's hip while on the ground | Horse willingly moves away from handler when the handler steps toward its hip |
| Forehand turn on the ground, haunch turn on the ground | Horse moves quietly away from the hand with minimal movement of the pivot foot |
| Backing the horse | Horse willingly gives to your body position and movement with minimal pressure on the lead rope / halter |
| Transition in the round pen, unsaddled | Horse moves through transitions based on the handler's foot and body movements and verbal cues |
| Hip disengagement while mounted | Horse performs the manuevers in both directions in a quiet and consistent manner |
| Forehand/haunch turn while mounted | Horse performs the maneuvers quietly due to consistent movement of rider's hands and legs |

| ACTION | HALLMARK REACHED |
|---|---|
| Correct and consistent riding | Horse and rider have developed a bond due to correct and consistent riding |
| Formation riding | Rider sends clear / concise messages to his mount, enabling the movements to be done correctly |
| Understanding the Key Insights | The Key Insights are the pre-stimulus training primer. A thorough knowledge of them is necessary for success |
| Towel test | Horse stands quietly while towel is draped around parts of his body |
| Noisy bag test | Horse stands quietly while being exposed to and bumped by the bag |
| Stepping over one or more ground poles | Horse moves willingly over poles without hitting the poles with its hooves |
| Crossing a wooden portable bridge | Horse consistently walks quietly over wooden bridge |
| Stimulus training | Horse accepts most items it faces. When frightnened, horse's actions are consistent, predictable and manageable |

Should communication break down between team members at any time during this systematic approach, either restart the system until success is enjoyed or tweak it to accommodate one or the other of the team members.

A word about confidence – confidence is a key component in this systems approach to bombproofing. Without the horse's confidence in the rider and the rider's confidence in the horse, the team will never progress past the initial steps of the system. However, the HSTS™ system is intended to build confidence for both members as goals and objectives (hallmarks) are met at each level.

## THE FIRST STEP IN THE HSTS™– GROUNDWORK IN AN ARENA

In this system, like any other, you have to begin at the beginning – groundwork. It does not matter if your horse is a three-year-old or an 18-year-old. It does not matter if the horse is brand new to you or you have owned it for years. If you intend to bombproof the animal, you begin the system with the horse unsaddled and in hand in a proper fitting halter and on a 10 to 12 foot lead rope.

We begin on the ground because it is critically important that the horse you are riding understands who is number one in the relationship. This realization can come at a great toll to both you and your mount if you begin on its back. On the ground, you can do a number of very simple maneuvers that will later translate into similar steps on the horse's back. These maneuvers, when done consistently and before riding, help to reinforce in the horse's mind that it is expected to respond to your cues. In other words, you are the General and he is the Private.

The intense nature of sensory training requires that the horse be totally responsive to the rider. The animal you are riding cannot be allowed the freedom to decide whether or not he will ignore your cues. The horse must be there for the rider at all times. It will only be there if the relationship is firmly established and the horse has confidence that the rider is not going to get it hurt.

In the herd hierarchy the position of the shoulder in relationship to other horses is important. Simply stated, the lead horse has dominated another horse whose body is behind his shoulder.

Christina is standing in a position of dominance. She is forward of Skippy's shoulder and pointing her toes toward the horse.

In order to test this theory, walk down a fairly wide road with a group of horses that are unknown to your mount. Put your horse in the lead position and notice the reaction when another horse begins to pass its shoulder. Depending on the individual animal, it might swing its head, pin its ears and may attempt to bite in order to keep the passing animal behind the shoulder. This is herd dominance in action. Therefore, when you have your horse in hand, unless you are doing a particular exercise, do not stand behind the shoulder of the horse you are holding. Standing in front of the horse's shoulder and facing the horse is just one more way to get the message across that you will not be dominated by this animal. The rider has successfully met a hallmark when he consistently stands in front of the horse's shoulder and squares up his body while facing his partner.

One of the most effective movements is to disengage the horse's hip. This maneuver is described in Chapter 2 as an important test to conduct before purchasing a horse. This procedure works from a psychological standpoint because the horse is being forced to move away from your body as you dominate its space. This maneuver is most effectively done when the horse learns to step through its mid-line, based not on being poked or prodded with your hand, but in time with the movement of your feet. When this is accomplished – and it takes consistent practice – there will be a major gain in establishing an effective relationship with the horse. As hip disengagements strengthen the hip, the trainer will have the added bonus of riding a more supple and athletic horse.

Horses are not inclined to back up if they have a choice. In the herd, they generally back only to avoid a kick or bite. By backing, they avoid a painful experience and allow themselves to be dominated. If they did not want to give in to the positional control of the horse that is dominant, they would move forward and challenge the aggressor.

Taking a horse in hand and causing it to move backwards away from you is an effective way to dominate its space. As you may remember reading in the Key Understandings, since horses speak space and position, you are talking volumes when you convince the horse to give to your position.

While backing the horse in hand, the bigger the leg and foot movements the easier it is for the horse to see them. Here Christina is dominating Skippy's space with her body movement.

The correct way to do this is to take the horse in hand, square it up and ask it to back by stepping into its space with your left or right foot. At the same time that you are asking by saying "back," you apply some pressure on the lead rope. As soon as you see the horse begin to shift its body, you relieve the hand pressure but maintain the foot in the air until the horse's corresponding front foot moves backwards. Initially you may need to touch with your toe just above the coronet band to get the horse to move his foot backwards.

Once the horse moves its first front foot, you continue walking toward the horse, applying slight pressure on the lead rope and asking it to back while stepping forward with the opposite foot. You have reached a hallmark when the horse gives in to you prior to your applying any pressure with the hand, and when lifting your foot causes the horse to quietly back up.

Turning on the forehand and the haunches as part of the groundwork are additional components to HSTS™. Both of these movements are used to reinforce the dominance of the human member of the team over his equine partner.

A turn on the haunches is performed by the horse turning around the inner hind leg. A turn on the forehand is performed by the horse turning around the inside foreleg.

A turn on the haunches to the right is accomplished by taking the lead rope in the left hand while standing facing the horse at the left shoulder. Pressure is applied down and toward the right with the left hand while pressing on the left shoulder of the horse with your right hand. You can also move your body into the horse to crowd its space while doing this. When the horse begins to give to the right, relieve the pressure on the rope but maintain the steady pressure on the shoulder. When the horse begins moving its feet, relieve the pressure on the shoulder. Press on the shoulder only until the horse shifts its weight and begins to lift the forefoot nearest to you. Move the horse 90 degrees and then let it rest.

Continue to do this 90 degrees at a time until you have completed a circle. When done properly, the left front foot of the horse should cross in front of its right front and its right rear becomes a pivot foot, staying in the same location throughout the movement. However, this level of expertise takes considerable practice. Do not forget to do the same movement from the other side of the horse, ensuring that its right front crosses over its left front and the left rear is the pivot foot.

A turn on the forehand from the ground requires that you apply pressure with your hand slightly behind where your heel would normally hang if you were in the saddle. For a turn on the forehand to the right, again grasp the lead rope, just below the snap, in your left hand while standing on the horse's left side. Move to the center of the horse and apply steady pressure with your hand on the horse's side at the location where your leg would normally make contact (or slightly behind that location) if you were mounted. Apply pressure on the lead rope by pulling slightly to the left or toward yourself. Maintain pressure on the horse's flank until it begins to shift the weight of its hip away from you or moves the hind foot that is closest to you. The horse should step in front of its right rear with its left rear and its left front is the pivot foot.

You have reached a hallmark with this maneuver when the horse readily moves away from you with minimal pressure on its flank and pivots quietly with only slight movement of the pivot foot.

## THE SECOND STEP IN HSTS™ – GROUNDWORK IN THE ROUND PEN

The round pen can be very useful in continuing the ground training of the horse. There are several absolutes when using a round pen. The round pen is the horse's equivalent of a classroom. Do not let the horse "goof off" while in class. Round pen work should be structured, simple and to the point. A few quality moments with positive accomplishments far outweighs mindless time spent running in circles. So keep the training focused and the horse's mind with you.

Putting the horse through speed transitions is one of the best uses of the round pen. By doing so we ensure the horse walks, trots and lopes on command going both directions. Many people accomplish this with the use of a whip. While that is one way to get it done, the use of the rider's body is a more effective tool in transition work. So put down that whip and pick up the horse's 10 to 12 foot lead rope.

Twirl the lead rope in the opposite hand from the direction you are asking the horse to move and begin to move your feet. Walk up toward the haunch of the horse, but be sure to keep your distance so it does not reach out and touch you with a hind foot. Ask for a gait in a voice the horse can hear. For a faster gait, get more aggressive with the rope, and move your feet faster while telling the horse the pace you want (jog, trot, lope, etc). When it moves off at the speed you want, slow down the rope, but keep your feet moving. You will soon notice how focused the horse is on the movement of your feet and how readily it will react to the speeding up or slowing down of your feet.

The hallmark for this movement is to eventually get the horse to move off in time with your feet and verbal cues without your having to twirl the lead rope.

Do not forget to do this in both directions and always quit on a good note, no matter how small a victory that may represent. There is an added bonus to this movement: you will get plenty of exercise while you and your horse are working in the round pen.

When you wish to have your horse change directions in the round pen, use your body to dominate its space. By moving from the back hip or haunch to the front shoulder and throwing up your hands or twirling the lead rope, the horse will turn away from you and change direction. An even easier method is to reverse yourself (a human version of a rollback) in order to meet the horse as it comes around. Upon meeting the horse, place the rope in the opposite hand you were using and raise it up to cause the horse to turn to the outside of the arena. To avoid injury to the horse, practice these movements at the walk and jog before going to the faster gaits.

One final word on round pen work. Since we never want to teach the horse anything incorrect while it is in school, do not let your horse lope off on the wrong lead. If it does so, immediately slow it down and try again.

You know you have reached a hallmark in this portion of HSTS™ when your horse will go through all gaits in both directions on the correct leads and at the correct speed by completely feeding off of your body movements and voice commands. That means that you no longer need to twirl a rope (and throw that whip away for heaven's sake) or aggressively move toward your horse to get it to cooperate. This takes time, but it is one of the most satisfying hallmarks you can reach!

## THE THIRD STEP OF HSTS™ –
## RIDING THE HORSE IN
### A Controlled Environment

As you can see, the system continues a natural progression to the next step, safely riding your partner in preparation for stimulus training. The most effective way to proceed is to perform the maneuvers that you have just done on the ground by mounting up on the horse's back. These initial movements are best done in a controlled environment, either a round pen or a smaller arena. Remember that as you ride this horse, the emphasis is on furthering the team relationship through communication that the horse understands.

### DISENGAGING THE HIP

One of the important movements you did on the ground was to disengage the horse's hip. It is an equally important maneuver to accomplish while on the horse. (Note: These movements are best accomplished in a ring snaffle bit.) Continue this while mounted by grasping the inside rein and putting the inside leg on the horse to support it through the ribcage. While holding the reins, place the inside hand on the inside knee. Allow some slack in the outside rein to allow the horse's head some freedom of movement. This movement, which is done at the walk, will cause the horse to turn to the inside and step through its mid-line with the inside rear leg. When you feel the horse step through three times, stop and reward it with a rub on the neck. Reverse directions, and repeat the movement.

Another way to accomplish this is to walk forward and raise your inside hand to about chest height and in line with the horse's spine. Maintain the hand in that position and support the horse with your inside leg. Allow a little slack in the outside rein so the horse can move its head to the inside. After the horse has stepped through its mid-line three times reward him by relieving the pressure and petting. Do the movement again walking in the other direction.

A hip disengagement to the left. Notice the big step through by the horse with its right rear leg.

It is important to stay centered and resist dropping your shoulder to the inside while the horse is stepping through. Shift your weight to the outside hip, keep your eyes and chin up and keep your lower back soft.

# BACKING

Once you have backed your horse on the ground, it is only natural to do so while mounted. Backing a horse is a matter of taking a deep seat, inhaling, asking the horse to "back" applying both legs to the horse's sides and exerting even pressure backwards on the reins. The key to getting the horse's cooperation is the timing of the hands and legs. Importantly, once you feel the horse begin to rock backwards in anticipation of taking that first step, relieve the pressure on the reins. In other words, immediately reward the horse for the step

it is taking. When this is done correctly, the hands pull and release in time with the backward movement of the horse.

Christina & Skippy are quietly backing up. To help this process, the rider has allowed a little upper body movement towards the withers of the horse thus freeing up the horse's hip.

Skippy continues backing - but not without protest as you can see by his tail movement.

56

Some horses are "sticky" at backing and can become extremely resistant to doing so. That is usually because of inexperience or more likely, bad experiences, such as being jerked in the face by a previous rider. If you can learn to give and take with the motion of the horse, the animal will appreciate your soft hands and give you those backward steps. It is also important that the horse back in a straight line. Therefore, when you feel its hind end veering to one side or the other, you must engage the appropriate leg in order to keep the horse straight. If you are unable to get your horse to consistently back up without resistance, dismount and redo the ground backing movements.

As a final thought on backing, sometimes you may need to quit when the horse has just given you one step when you really wanted five steps. That may have to suffice because it is always better to stop on a positive note than to set up a fight that you may not be able to win!

## TURNS ON THE FOREHAND AND HAUNCHES

Turning the horse on the forehand and haunces are both important components of the HSTS™ process. They are quiet, slow and controlled movements that, when properly done, speak volumes to your mount.

One of the best methods to begin this process is to insure that your horse is moving quietly off your leg. Line your horse up on the rail facing the inside of the arena. Walk him quietly to the other side. Just before getting to the arena fence, shorten your left rein by lifting your left hand so you can see your horse's eye and apply your left leg to the horse. Your horse will step through with its left rear leg and pivot slightly on its left front foot. Ask the horse to stop and it should end up standing parallel with the fence.

Do this same movement heading the other direction and turning the opposite direction you just completed. Continue doing this a number of times until you get the timing of the hands and legs down, and the horse is moving off your legs with ease. Then kick it up a notch and perform these movements at a trot. Obviously, with the faster pace, timing is even more critical. Once you have accomplished turns in both directions at the trot, it is time to move to the next two hallmarks: haunch and forehand turns.

To do a turn on the forehand to the right, shorten your left rein and apply your left leg slightly behind the natural fall of your foot. Maintain pressure with the leg until you begin to feel the horse shift its weight. Then relieve the pressure. Continue the "press and release" with the movement of the horse's left rear leg until you have moved 90 degrees. Reward the horse with a rub,

Christina is now setting Skippy up for a turn on the forehand. Note that she will be moving his rear end to the horse's right – so she has helped this process by ensuring Skippy's left rear is slightly ahead of the right rear.

The movement begins – you can see some resistance in Skippy's body language as the horse's head is a little high. However, he is stepping through nicely with his left rear.

Skippy is beginning to relax a little as his head has started to drop. He continues to step through with the left hind. Notice that Christina has shortened up her left rein to help the horse with his weight distribution.

then continue the process until you are able to do a complete circle. Practice this in the opposite direction by making the necessary hand and leg changes.

For a haunch turn to the right (which means the shoulder of your horse is going to move to the right) shorten your right rein slightly (just so you can see your horse's right eye) and apply your left leg at the cinch or slightly forward of the cinch. Reward the horse with relief from your foot pressure when it begins the

Here, Christina is setting Skippy up for a turn on the haunch. Note that the horse is "squared up" before attempting this manuever.

Christina and Skippy begin the movement by moving to the right. Notice Christina's body position which allows the horse freedom in his right shoulder to make the movement. She is also pushing with her left leg and allowing the horse to step through her right leg. She is guiding the horse with her right hand and rein. Skippy is doing a great cross over in the front.

The movement continues and Christina is working hard not to get in the way of the horse.

movement. Maintain lightness with your hands so the horse does not back up and has the freedom to step over his right front foot with his left front foot. Again do 90 degrees, reward the horse, then, after completing the full circle, go the other direction. If the horse is "sticky" or very stubborn, dismount and remind it how the movements are done while on the ground. Then remount and try again.

BE SATISFIED WITH LITTLE VICTORIES
AND ALWAYS QUIT ON A GOOD NOTE!

## THE FOURTH PHASE OF HSTS™ – RIDING OUTSIDE THE ARENA

Once you have mastered the techniques inside an arena, the next step is to move outside in a flat, safe area where the horse has good footing. The movements are essentially the same. The difference is that you no longer have the arena rails to use as a "crutch." Some horses also display a less willing attitude when they know they are not constrained. So it is important to complete this part of the system.

After you have successfully accomplished the first four phases of the HSTS™, you can have confidence that your horse will be more willing during the challenging stimulus course portion of the training discussed later in this book.

# Third Lesson Learned

No matter how "bombproof" your horse may be, do not try to force him through an obstacle by attaching a rope to another horse and pulling your horse forward.

Several years ago we were sponsoring a joint training day with a number of Southern California Mounted Units. One of the obstacles we designed was a "water trap." A water trap is a hole dug in the ground with a tarp laid over the hole. It is then filled with water. It is a challenging obstacle for even the best of horses. Once a couple of horses go through the trap, dirt is mixed with the water and it darkens. The horse has no way of knowing if the water is shallow or deep. Because of this, many horses want no part of the trap. Rather than take a chance of stepping into it they will either shy away or attempt to jump it.

On this particular day, we were amazed when our best mounted horse, Rikki, who had worked with the unit for over 10 years, balked at the trap. In fact, he would not get within several feet of the water-filled hole. So, the decision was made to lead him through with a horse that had already success-fully accomplished the obstacle. With the rider still aboard, the lead rider and horse "dallied up" a lead rope and began to pull Rikki toward the trap. Instead of walking forward, Rikki stood straight up and dumped the rider. In fact, he almost went over backwards on top of the officer who was lying flat on his back in the arena.

At the moment this happened, a picture was taken and, to this day, Rikki looks like he is doing an imitation of a rocket ship at the moment of launch. Fortunately, no one was seriously injured and we all learned an important lesson.

# CHAPTER 4

# The Importance of Equitation in Sensory Training

The fifth component of the Horse Sensory Training System™ is riding your horse. Sounds simple enough – but it is often an area in which people are remiss in truly getting the training accomplished. One of the greatest drawbacks to being successful in bombproofing your horse can be called the "motorcycle mentality." In other words, you "park" the animal and then expect it to perform when you show up once a month to ride. Unlike a motorcycle, a horse cannot stand for days on end and then be successfully driven off after sticking a key in the ignition and firing it up. Instead, successful riding, and therefore, bombproofing, takes proper practice and consistency to reach success.

Have you ever tried to get someone to define equitation for you? Depending on the person you ask, you will get a variety of answers. Most will be descriptions of what good equitation should look like, depending on the discipline that particular person rides. The dictionary simply calls it the art of horse riding. Perhaps we could expand on that by saying that it is the art of influencing a horse through proper position of the rider.

# The Correct Riding Position

Correct positioning is important for three reasons. The first is so the aids can be applied in a consistent manner. Horses learn through repetition. Your legs, seat, and hands must be in the same place each time you ask for a specific movement. For example, to ask your horse to trot from the walk (with your weight squarely in the saddle and your hands in front of your hips), you simply press your legs against its sides until the horse trots. What if the next time you wanted to trot, you closed your legs but leaned back in the saddle or pulled back on the reins? How would your horse know that you wanted it to trot? Your aids were not in the same place. You were not consistent and this confuses your horse.

The second reason for correct position is balance. It is important to stay centered on your horse. When you lean either forward, backward or sideways, you throw off the horse's balance and you are unbalanced while on its back. This can be critical in sensory training. It is not unusual for a horse to make a rapid movement during the training. If you are not centered on the horse, you will be spending the next several minutes dusting yourself off!

Unbalanced riding will quickly fatigue your horse as it struggles to carry you and maintain its balance as well. I like to use the analogy of giving a child a piggyback ride. Everyone knows how difficult it is to carry a squirming child or one who is leaning to one side. It is no different for your horse. I have seen horses that were actually permanently crooked from years of carrying an unbalanced rider.

The third reason for good position is you will be visually pleasing. Looking good in the saddle is important for all riders. Get in the habit of always practicing good posture because you are probably being watched.

It should be fairly obvious how vital good equitation is to everyone who rides a horse. The ideal mount is instantly obedient and tuned in to its rider's slightest cue. This precision is only achieved through correct and consistent application of the aids, which is a product of balance and position.

So just what is this "proper position?" Looking at the rider from the side, it is the vertical alignment of the shoulder, hip and heel. As the rider is sitting in the saddle, an imaginary line drawn from the ear to the ground would intersect those three points. The elbows are bent so that the upper arm lies along the torso and there is a straight line from the elbow to the horse's mouth. The thumbs are turned up and point to the horse's ears, and the fingers are gently closed around the reins. The heels are slightly down in the stirrups. The rider's eyes are looking ahead, not at the ground or the horse's ears. The back is straight without being stiff. There is no arch in the lower back or slump in the shoulders. Looking at the rider from the back, the shoulders and hips should be horizontal or parallel to the ground. There should be no collapsing of either shoulder or hip and no leaning to one side.

## Developing the Seat

Does all of this have your head spinning? It really is not as difficult as it sounds. You do not have to be a contortionist to achieve a natural, correct position. If you do not have access to mirrors when you ride, and most of us do not, then you may need some eyes on the ground to help get you into the correct position.

If you have been riding for a while in the wrong position, the initial corrections will feel awkward. Work with a professional trainer or, lacking that person, enlist the help of a friend to tell you if your heels are lined up under your shoulders or if your elbows are bent.

It is very common to develop riding habits that you are completely unaware of. You may even adamantly deny doing them. Yet, your trainer can spot them immediately and make corrections. Also, consider using a video camera. Have someone tape your ride. Take a deep breath and then watch the video. You will probably see some flaws that you didn't know existed and you can then work toward correcting them.

One of the best ways to develop a good seat is to be lunged while riding. Enlist a professional to help you because this can be a bit tricky if your helper has never lunged a horse. (An experienced horse is also a good idea. Use a school horse if yours is green.)

In this exercise, which should be done in a round pen, the rider only has to concentrate on his position because the horse is under the control of the trainer. This allows the rider to focus on his seat, legs, weight and hands without worrying about steering the horse.

A lot can be accomplished in a very short time with this training technique.

Once you have experienced the correct position a time or two, you can begin to develop muscle memory and can recreate the feeling or correct position on your own.

You are off to a good start. But now what? Are you afraid to move for fear of sacrificing your hard-earned position? The next step is to learn to maintain the basics while in motion. The faster the gait, the quicker everything happens and the easier it is to lose your balance. The best way to become a fluid rider is simply, to coin an old phrase, a lot of wet saddle blankets! In other words, get on your horse and ride. Take long rides, short rides, ride in the arena, or on the trail. Practice riding wherever and whenever you can. This is not an endeavor that one can learn in a couple of afternoons. It takes many hours in the saddle and lots of commitment. For some in our society, it is a lifelong passion!

## Dressage Riding

Along with that commitment, you need a game plan. There must be a logical progression that horse and rider can follow – a process that leads to the finished product. An excellent foundation for all other forms of riding is the art of classical dressage. This type of training teaches the horse obedience and suppleness. It improves the balance of both horse and rider. Dressage increases your ability to move in harmony with your horse. Your mount learns to respond more to seat and leg aids and can achieve self-carriage, which is much less tiring for everyone.

The benefits of dressage training are many and varied. The great cavalry units of Europe readily recognized these benefits. Some components of dressage are still employed by the riding instructors of the Royal Canadian Mounted Police in readying their officers for the famous Musical Ride.

Dressage training is very systematic. This is an asset because it eliminates the guesswork. There are several levels of competition, from Training Level to Grand Prix riding. At each level, the expectations of the horse are clearly defined and as horse and rider progress through the levels, the degree of difficulty increases.

This allows the horse to be taught in a logical manner, with more challenging moves added only after certain basics have been mastered.

Even if you have absolutely no intention of ever showing dressage, there is much to be learned by examining the requirements at each level and following the basic plan. I do not mean to imply that every horse be trained in exactly the same manner. Each horse is an individual and that must be taken into account. However, a basic training outline is definitely beneficial to both horse and rider.

Dressage training also demands discipline from the rider. You are not going to progress unless you are practicing several times a week. So, if you really want to get that perfect "shoulder-in" or "half-pass" or whatever it is you are striving for, you need to be on your horse and be focused on your goals. Simply strolling down the trail daydreaming is certainly fine every so often, but will not do much to improve your riding skills unless, perhaps, your horse kicks up a nest of angry bees!

Becoming more serious about your riding offers more than one advantage. Not only do your skills improve but the bond between you and your horse will become stronger. A strong partnership cannot be underestimated in successfully bombproofing your horse.

Kris Seals on Gator, obviously happy with their performance.

Any horse can benefit from dressage training. I believe this so firmly that I am going to repeat it

Any Horse Can Benefit from Dressage Training!

You do not have to own an expensive warmblood to ride the exercises and patterns that are used in dressage. While some horses have conformation that makes it easier to collect, extend or get their haunches under them, any horse can perform the movements.

Who would argue that they do not want their horse to be more obedient, more balanced and easier to ride? It doesn't even matter what type of tack you use. You can achieve lasting results through classical dressage training in that old funky western saddle you have been riding for years. You do, however, need to ride in a snaffle bit for the best results.

## The Six Steps
## of Dressage Schooling

I have focused on why dressage is so effective. Now, let's move on to how it works. Once you have established forward momentum in your horse – so that it moves willingly off your lightly-squeezed leg – you can begin working on what is referred to as the training scale. This scale consists of six steps that guide the ride and ultimately produce a well-trained mount.

The first step is rhythm. Your horse must be able to maintain a steady rhythm in each of its gaits. You can change the tempo or steps per minute, but the rhythm must remain steady.

The second step in the training scale is relaxation. A relaxed horse is listening to the rider, has a swinging back and is easy to turn in both directions. There is a lack of tension in its major muscle groups and the head carriage reflects that fact.

Relaxation, combined with rhythm, helps the horse to achieve the third step, contact. If the horse is being ridden forward in a regular rhythm with big swinging steps, then it can achieve balance. The horse will feel confident enough to take contact on the bit. How much contact will differ from horse to horse. Some like more contact than others. The horse's level of training also affects the amount of contact you can establish.

Fourth on the scale is "impulsion." The horse is using its hind quarters to push forward, creating power that is channeled through the back and into the bit. A horse with impulsion has some "spring" to its gaits.

Once your horse is moving forward in an energetic, rhythmical manner and is responsive to your steering aids, you can begin to straighten it. Straightness is the fifth item on the training scale. This means that the horse's hind feet are traveling in the same path as its front feet. Most horses need help in this department, as they are all naturally crooked to some degree. To straighten a horse, the rider must move the front-end over to align with the back-end. Only then can the horse balance and truly step through from behind.

These five steps are used together like a recipe to create a balanced ride. This recipe can change; it is not set in stone. One day, you may need to work more on rhythm. The next day, the rhythm is fine but the impulsion is lacking. Yet another day, your horse may not seem very supple at first, but suddenly you realize that you weren't riding straight. When you fix that problem, the horse will relax and seek the natural balance you create – the proper mix of rhythm, relaxation, contact, impulsion and straightness.

After succeeding in the first five steps, you can move on to collection – the sixth and last step on the training scale. Collection occurs when the horse's hindquarters carry more of its weight and the forehand lightens. This is also known as self-carriage.

These six steps of the training scale will help guide you through a gradual training system for your horse. Every time you ride, check to see if one of these steps is missing. If so, you must regain it. When combined with correct position in the saddle, even the most difficult movement will now come more easily to the forward-thinking horse.

"This guy wants me to ride Dressage – won't I look funny doing that in my cowboy hat?" Well, the point is that Dressage offers some real advantages to those who want to sensory train their horses. If you do not see yourself doing this, then pick another discipline that more closely fits your viewpoint and practice it consistently. This is best done with a professional instructor, but that is not absolutely necessary. In today's world there are numerous books and videos that will take you from A-Z in any riding discipline you can imagine. Avail yourself of those resources.

Ultimately, good riding and horsemanship are good riding and horsemanship no matter what discipline you ride. All riding disciplines have common denominators involving eyes, hands, balance, aids and body position.

Most importantly, your horse must be comfortable with you. If you have not developed a bond through consistent and correct riding skills, your horse will not have the confidence it takes to succeed at stimulus training.

The ability to work comfortably in a round pen or an arena is fundamental to sensory training. Many people and some horses are adverse to arena work of any kind. If this is your case, you may need to change your thinking and accept that the control offered by those rails will make the difference between success and failure.

# Fourth Lesson Learned

Watch out for ropes while doing sensory training.

Several years ago, one of our mounted officers was significantly injured while doing sensory training with the "noisy can drag." The noisy can drag is a gunnysack filled with aluminum cans or plastic bottles attached to a long rope. The idea behind this obstacle is for the rider to take the rope in hand and drag the sack on the ground towards him while the horse is facing the bag. The rider expects the horse to stand quietly, watching the bag as it comes toward him.

In this particular incident, when the rider pulled the bag the horse turned away from it and the rope was caught up under the skirt of the saddle. The noisy can bag jumped toward the horse, which elicited a further reaction from the horse. It all went down hill from there.

The horse, now thinking it was being attacked by the bag, continued spinning away until the rider was unseated.

A broken wrist was the result of this accident.

Another Rope Story

We used to ride during training with halters and lead ropes on the horses. The lead rope was attached with a snap to the halter and tied off at the

76

saddle horn. One day, during sensory training, a horse reared up and came down with the lead rope of the horse standing next to him between his front legs.

Now this is a wreck!

The weight of the horse that reared pushing down on the lead rope began to cause the second horse to go down. At the same time, the horse with the rope between its legs began to lunge violently, trying to get free. Fortunately, the rider of horse number two had a very sharp knife and managed to cut his lead rope, thus freeing the other animal.

Amazingly, other than a slight rope burn between the horse's front legs, there was no other injury to either man or beast that day.

The lesson learned: when dealing with horses, no matter what you are doing, always carry a sharp knife that can be used at a moment's notice.

CHAPTER 5

# The Basics of Formation Riding

One of the important components of the Horse Sensory Training System™ is formation riding. In the United States, formation riding finds its roots in the movements of the U.S. Cavalry. By modifying the already established movements, police departments were able to apply them to many things they do on a daily basis, especially in managing crowds.

## The Importance of Formation Riding

Most people do not understand the importance of teaching horses to work together as part of an organized group. Formation riding teaches discipline for both the horse and rider and has a significant impact on the ability to accomplish further sensory training. Formation riding is a component of sensory training. It is not a normal part of the average day of horseback riding, and can be very stressful to the average equine.

One of the reasons formation riding is essential is it takes a great deal of concentration from both the horse and rider. It requires attention to detail and the ability of the rider to communicate instantaneous demands to his equine partner. These demands must be instantly obeyed or the formation can quickly become unstrung. Because formation riding can be such an intense experience, horse and rider must truly become a team – each understanding and reacting to the other's communications.

Formation riding requires the complete attention of each individual rider as well as the person in charge of the formation (Officer In Charge, or OIC). This concentration is translated into discipline as riders work with their horses to ensure that they are performing the correct movement. Without this inherent discipline, there will be little success, particularly when movements are done at a gait faster than a walk.

There are a number of things that can be learned about your horse through formation riding. Perhaps the most important is how aggressive your mount will be toward others in the herd. Unfortunately, in today's world many horses are raised isolated or corralled in a box. These horses never have an opportunity to interact in a herd. They miss that very important socialization process that goes on in the herd, even if it is just a herd of two or three horses.

This lack of social interaction creates a high degree of anxiety for a horse when it is suddenly thrust into the mix during formation riding, a trail ride or other horse event. This anxiety becomes manifest in a number of what humans consider to be anti-social behaviors, such as kicking, biting or striking. At the least, a horse that has not had herd interaction in its lifetime will be very hesitant to stand quietly with other animals in a basic formation. In fact, its reactions may closely resemble those of a horse that is claustrophobic. Though the reason for this claustrophobia, however, is not necessarily due to an inherent closed-in feeling, but rather concern over where the horse fits into the herd. Often, the horse will continually attempt to back out of a line of horses or swing its head and threaten those that are standing next to it. With continuous practice and correction, both of these negative habits can be eradicated.

Many of us ride horses that are insistent upon a certain location in the herd while going on a trail ride. Some of us own or have seen a horse that will jig during a ride until he gets to the front of the herd. Or perhaps your horse is the one that fails to keep up – constantly lagging in the back and wearing out your legs in the process. Formation riding goes a long way in correcting these behaviors. During this process, horses are constantly changing their locations "in the herd" and soon lose interest in trying to maintain a particular position in the formation.

The horse soon realizes that the effort expended to maintain its preferred position is not worth it because it may be changing locations as often as six or eight times in one minute. Additionally, because of the intensity of formation riding, riders work harder to control their mounts through more consistent communications. Failure to do so can cause embarrassment to a rider and we all know to what extent humans will go in order to avoid being embarrassed.

There are some important basics to formation riding:

- Formation riding enhances communications between horse and rider

- The slower paces, even working from the halt, must be mastered first

- It takes consistent work and practice in order to do it right

- Persons giving formation commands must do so in a clear, concise and consistent manner

While formation riding can get very complex, there are some basic movements that help to establish an important relationship, which are key components of the HSTS.™

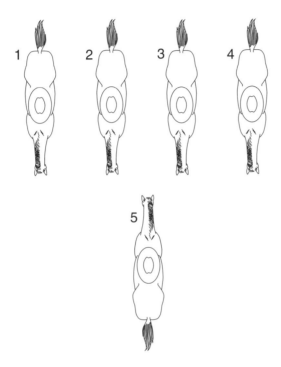

### Troop Front

The troop front is the basic assembly formation. It consists of a line of horses – riders sitting stirrup to stirrup facing the Officer In Charge (OIC). If one walks to either end of the line and looks down it, the saddle horns should be in perfect alignment. This alignment is accomplished by "covering down" to the right by ensuring that your shoulder is even with the person to your immediate right.

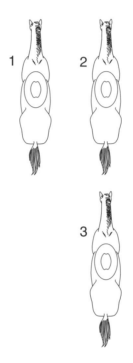

## Column of Twos

The column of twos is the primary way to move a formation of riders. In a column of twos, horse spacing is four feet nose to tail and one foot stirrup to stirrup. The column of twos is important because many other movements are done using this formation as a starting place. A single rider in a column of twos always rides to the right and behind the last pair.

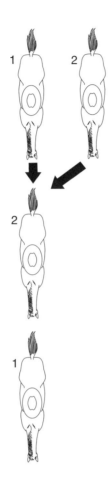

## Single File

Placing horses in a single file is also a way to move from one location to another. However, the lead horse must be very brave because it is literally walking point and must be willing to move forward consistently. Horses in a single file should be two feet apart nose to tail.

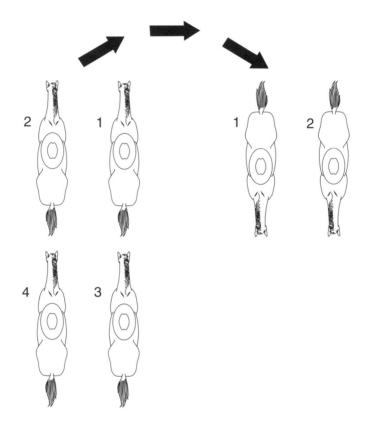

## Roundabouts

Roundabouts, which are done either to the left, right or center, are effective ways to have a column of twos change directions. Doing roundabouts allows the OIC to maintain the same two lead riders.

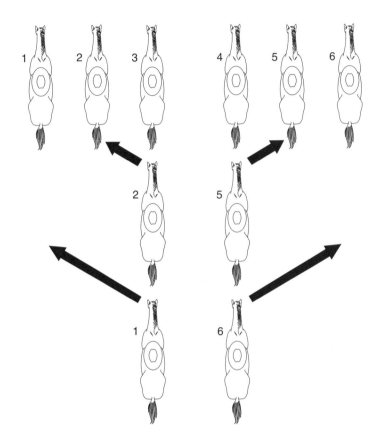

## On-Line Movements

On-line movements are used to get a column of twos into a line of horses. Thus, an on-line movement can be to the left, right or center of the column, depending on the need of the formation. This graphic shows an "on-line" center.

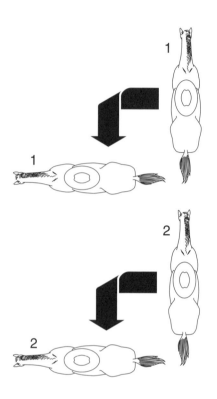

## Flanking Movements

A flanking movement is used to change the direction of a line of horses 90 degrees. It is best accomplished from a single file. When the riders hear the command of "to the right flank, move," they each turn crisply 90 degrees and ride to a location across from them (i.e. a particular fence post). While riding, they maintain their spacing between the other riders and continually check to ensure they are in line (covered down) to the right.

All commands for formation movements consist of a preparatory command ("to the rear") and a command of execution ("move" or "yo"). By doing the commands in this manner, the rider has a moment to think about and prepare for the upcoming movement. Once the riders hear the command of execution, they perform the movement in unison. This gives a polished and crisp appearance.

One final word on formation riding: With sufficient practice, it can be done at all gaits. Therefore, it is a good way to burn up some excess energy before approaching a sensory course.

# Fifth Lesson Learned

As obvious as this may sound, it needs to be said as a reminder to anyone who is contemplating sensory training. Always inspect your riding equipment before beginning the training.

There is nothing better than a game of tag at the end of a day of training horses when you are in a group. Tag allows the riders and horses to unwind from the stresses and strains of the training. Tag also continues to reinforce some of the lessons learned on any given day – lessons such as centered riding, using your aids and connecting with your horse. The added competition found in the game helps to sharpen many of these skills. However, tag is absolutely no fun if you have failed to inspect your equipment and tighten up your cinch before playing.

In 1998 we were wrapping up a full training day with a neighboring agency when the challenge went out for a game of tag. Our riders, who were perhaps more familiar with the downfalls (literally) of not checking the cinch prior to this game, were careful to "cinch up" before starting. The members of the other department did not perform this simple step before the competition began. Approximately halfway through the game, and while at a full gallop, the head trainer for the other team attempted a quick evasive maneuver. Had it worked, it would have been poetry in motion.

Unfortunately, the cinch was loose and the saddle rolled with the rider going completely underneath the horse. Now at a full gallop, this is a place you would rather not be!

The good news was that the horse managed to move over the rider without touching her with his feet. Of course, he was less forgiving of the saddle hanging from his belly and was quick to kick it into pieces. The trainer was extremely embarrassed, but otherwise unhurt.

The lesson learned – inspect your equipment and be sure to check that cinch before doing sensory training.

# CHAPTER 6

# Key Insights into Sensory Training

There are 11 key insights concerning the sensory training of your horse that must be explored before attempting the stimulus portion of the actual training. Being clear on these insights can make the difference between a fruitful training day or a total wreck.

## KEY INSIGHT #1

Safety has to be the first consideration. During sensory training, riders may experience unexpected reactions from their mounts. It is not uncommon for horses to employ a number of avoidance maneuvers to include spinning, bolting, quickly backing, rearing or bucking or, for the very challenging animal, all of the above. Because of this, when exposing horses to sensory stimuli, which is the sixth step in the HSTS™, everything possible should be done to prevent injury to riders and horses alike.

Stimulus exposure must be done in an arena to control the possibility of a runaway (close the gate!). The footing should be very good and the arena should be soft sand or plowed dirt that is free of rocks. A first aid kit and access to a telephone are absolutely required.

Personal riding equipment should include boots with a heel, a riding helmet and a sharp knife that can be opened with one hand. Spurs should be worn only if the rider has used them consistently on his mount. (Note: Stimulus exposure is not the time to try out new equipment. You want that mount as comfortable as possible in the old tried and true equipment.)

It is very difficult to do any type of sensory training without help and it should never be done alone while mounted. There is too much potential for something to go wrong. Most horses do better at sensory training when there are other horses in the arena.

When training with a number of horses and riders, one person should be assigned to oversee safety. This should be an experienced horse person who recognizes when a rider is headed for trouble. The overseer must be equipped with a whistle and "blow dead" the action if there is a problem. Upon hearing the whistle, all activity in the arena immediately stops until the emergency is resolved.


## KEY INSIGHT #2

During sensory training, the horse must win! There is no alternative that will provide the animal with the motivation to continue trying. When exposing horses to sensory stimulus, it is very easy to psychologically overexpose the animal and cause a blow-up. This is completely counterproductive to what you are trying to accomplish.

As an example, if you are attempting to get a horse to walk across a plywood board, you do not "pour the spurs" to it or whip the animal until it finally steps on the board. It is highly likely that effort will result in the horse doing something other than stepping on the wood. And the something other may be an attempt to jump the wood or rear up and dump the rider. The correct way to accomplish this is to cue the horse forward, allow him to put his head down and examine the wood and relax. What's the hurry?

Remember Key Understanding # 1 – your horse does not think like you do. It does not know it is only a piece of plywood, so the horse needs some time to digest the obstacle before being pressured into crossing it. Give it that time. After the horse has settled, cue it forward. After one or two steps, let it take another look. Continue this process until the horse realizes that the item it is examining is benign. Eventually, with the right amount of patience and coaxing, most horses will walk across the piece of plywood.

If your horse continues to balk at crossing the plywood, try using a "mother horse" to get it across. A mother horse is an animal that is willing and able to complete the obstacle. When the resistant animal sees another walk across the plywood and nothing happens, often it will follow suit.

Part of allowing the horse to win is knowing when to say "when." Perhaps the closest you will get to that scary plywood in the first go around is within several feet. That may have to be good enough. Leave that piece of plywood, let the horse unwind and move to a different obstacle. Or take a break and try again later. Usually, you will be able to get closer and closer until the horse completes the challenge.

Never spend more than three to four minutes at any one obstacle if you are not reaching some measure of improvement. Never dismount and attempt to pull a horse across a ground obstacle. This is very dangerous. It can cause severe injury when your 1,100-pound animal jumps into your lap. It is also not a good idea to have another rider "dally up" and attempt to pull the horse across while you are either mounted or dismounted. In this situation, the horse is not being allowed to win. It is just being forced to do something it obviously is not in a frame of mind to accomplish.

## KEY INSIGHT #3

Horses learn best through positive and consistent repetition. This is particularly true in the world of sensory training because failure to control the training takes away its positive nature. That is why allowing the horse to win is so critical in this process.

## KEY INSIGHT #4

Control your ego, control your temper and do not over-ride the abilities of your horse. Many wrecks are related to the human's need to conquer an obstacle before the horse is ready to assist. This is usually a result of the natural competitiveness of humans, which, if unchecked, can cause the loss of temper. There is absolutely no room in this process for a person who loses his temper because his mount balks at an obstacle.

One of the cornerstones of HSTS™ is that the horse wins at each obstacle. If it is being spurred, whipped and otherwise worked over, the horse definitely does not feel like a winner. It may relate the abuse to the obstacle, which only makes it that much more difficult to get the horse through it in the future. Persons who are sensory training their horses must be satisfied with little victories depending on the personality of the horse they are riding. Horses, like humans, learn at different rates. Each individual animal must be given the freedom to score accomplishments at its own pace.

## KEY INSIGHT #5

Understand the role of both self-discipline and discipline for your mount in this process. Horses that are successfully sensory trained must have a high degree of discipline in order to accomplish the training. In today's world of kinder, gentler training, there is still the need to discipline the animal that is displaying anti-social behavior. The trick in disciplining a horse is knowing what force is appropriate and the timing of the use of the selected force.

Timing is easier. When disciplining an animal, your reaction needs to be almost instantaneous with the transgression or at least within a few seconds. Knowing what level of force to use depends on the animal. Horses have varying degrees of sensitivity to correction. Some will instantly understand a transgression with a stern verbal warning; others will require some degree of force to get the message across.

It is important to use the force appropriate to the transgression. Thus, we do not hit a horse with a whip because he is slow to learn or spooks and unloads us during a ride. And, with one exception, never hit a horse around its face. The exception is if the animal is charging you with a face full of teeth or has bitten you. Horse bites (not nips by young horses) are the ultimate in disrespect. They can result in serious and permanent injury and must be dealt with drastically.

Ultimately, each rider must determine what is appropriate for their mount when they are considering discipline options.

Human self-discipline is also an important part of sensory training. This comes in the form of maintaining one's temper, reassuring the horse when appropriate and having the personal courage to successfully challenge each obstacle. These are imperative considerations and can mean the difference between success and failure in the bombproofing process.

## KEY INSIGHT #6

The sensory obstacles presented must be appropriate to the horse's maturity, psychological strength and training level. One does not attempt to put a very young horse over a water obstacle, especially if the horse has never waded across a creek. In a group of horses, this may present challenges, as some horses will be more willing and more confident than others. However, it is important to forego the challenge that a horse is totally unequipped to handle. It is better to let that animal "sit it out" on the sidelines, or view the obstacle from a comfortable distance, than risk a wreck. Remember that the goal is to allow the animal to win, which it can only do if it is psychologically capable of handling the stimulus.

## KEY INSIGHT #7

The more frequently you do sensory training, the better the horse will get. Remember Key Understanding #8 – horses never forget. You can bet that they always remember the bad things that happen to them, especially if they get hurt. But horses also never forget that they can be successful. Otherwise we would not be able to ride them. If your horse is allowed to win, is not injured during the training and is not overloaded by overriding, the next time it faces sensory training, you will be amazed at what the horse can accomplish. This is even true of horses that only get significant sensory training once a year. They will continue to improve and readily accept a variety of obstacles with more and more ease.

## KEY INSIGHT #8

Using patterns of consistency through employing the entire HSTS™ will bring success. Again, it is the system that is important – starting with groundwork, riding in a controlled environment, riding outside the controlled environment and finally working up to the scariest obstacle imaginable. Failing to fully reach a hallmark at each step of the system will lengthen the time needed. It may even preclude a rider from accomplishing the bombproofing. Each step is important in the overall accomplishment of the goal. Applying the steps consistently in a pattern is also critical. One does not do the riding before the groundwork or the stimulus training before the riding. Each step has its time and place in the system.

## KEY INSIGHT #9

Take your time. For the average person who is not involved in law enforcement, bombproofing does not have to be accomplished in a compressed time frame. Do not be in a hurry. Master each of the movements in HSTS™ and reach those hallmarks before moving on. Not only will you have a horse that will be more easily sensory trained, but you will find your mount to be more willing and a better partner no matter what your riding goals.

## KEY INSIGHT #10

Do not override your own abilities. Be realistic about what type of rider you are and how balanced and centered you are in the saddle. As you may recall from the equitation portion of this book, centered riding is critical to the completion of sensory training. Some horses will make a variety of sudden movements during sensory training. Therefore, a rider who is not centered may become easily dismounted. The bottom line for maintaining your seat during sensory training is closely related to the experience level of the rider. While all riders have the potential to be successful, those with many years of riding experience and/or professional riding instruction have an edge up for accomplishing the goals.

## KEY INSIGHT #11

Check and double-check your equipment before stimulus training. Be sure it fits properly, is not unduly worn, the cinch is tight, the bit is properly placed in the mouth and you are otherwise ready to go. If you are in a group of people, this is the time for an inspection of the equipment for fit, wear, utility and comfort for the horse. A pre-stimulus training equipment check is as vital to the rider as a pre-flight check is to a pilot.

# Sixth Lesson Learned

Sensory training, when done right, builds confidence between the horse and rider. When done incorrectly, it has the opposite effect. In essence it can tear down what little confidence the team may have.

Several years ago, we had an officer and his mount that were fairly new to the mounted unit. At the time, we were into extreme sensory training, often at the expense of other training needs such as equitation. Unfortunately, while training this new team, instead of building confidence, we were in effect dismantling it.

Most horses improve over time if the sensory training presented is compatible with the psychological strength of the horse. However, in our zeal to produce horses that would withstand any type of stimulus they may encounter on the street, we forgot this crucial lesson. In this particular case, the horse and rider began a downward spiral which revolved around loss of confidence. One day, we totally overloaded the horse and it bucked off the rider. While the rider was not seriously injured, he loaded up his horse and essentially told us that we had no clue as to what we were doing. In hindsight, I know that he was correct.

The officer and his horse never again came to train, which was a shame because he was a very capable officer, a good rider and had a horse that would have excelled at the job. Unfortunately, through our training, the horse had lost confidence in the rider and the rider had lost confidence in both the horse and the training process.

After this event, we re-evaluated our training methods and took the lesson learned to heart. In the many years since, this scenario has not been repeated.

# CHAPTER 7

# Putting it all Together –
# Doing Stimulus Training

Since the ultimate goal for bombproofing the horse is a solid, steady and reliable mount, there comes a time when the entire Horse Sensory Training System™ is melded together to accomplish that goal. HSTS™ ends with the actual hands-on stimulus training that has been talked about so frequently in this book.

Before embarking on the stimulus training, everyone needs to do a reality check concerning the horse they are riding. This needs to be an honest assessment of the horse and its ability to accomplish this potentially difficult process. Does this animal, no matter what its age, have what it takes to be successful? Or will the stress of stimulus training be too much for its fragile psyche?

In the world of police horse training, anywhere from 25 to 50 percent of the horses are washed out during stimulus training. Therefore, it is very possible that the horse you are riding may not be successful. Because you control the level of training and the degree of accomplishment in this system and because you are following the HSTS,™ failure is less likely. But, even this does not absolutely guarantee success. In fact it may ultimately help a rider to realize that his horse is unlikely to succeed. This knowledge can lead to a reevaluation of the horse's potential for completing stimulus training.

There are two critical things that you will learn during stimulus training. One is what your mount will react to and the second is what that reaction will be.

In the world of horses, it is unrealistic to expect no reaction to startling events. After all, if someone walks up behind you and drops a firecracker at your feet, you will react! It is the same for the horse. Through this system, riders will learn what will cause a reaction in their mounts.

Many horses will accept a wide variety of stimuli such as balls being thrown at them, smoke grenades, fireworks, sirens – you name it. All horses have something that will get their attention. It is important for the rider to know what "that something" is. This allows the rider to anticipate and correct the reaction and spend time working on desensitizing the horse to this fear.

Knowing the mode of an individual horse's reaction is just as important as knowing what will cause a reaction. Therefore, if your horse consistently spins to the left when it refuses to walk on the piece of plywood, (or is faced with any other unknown obstacle) the rider can anticipate that reaction and make corrections to get the horse to face that which it fears. If your horse bucks or rears when faced with new challenges, perhaps that animal is not ready for the training or may never be ready for sensory training.

One of the most difficult horses to deal with is the one that reacts differently each time it is frightened.

Therefore, a horse which displays predictable reactions when frightened is more easily sensory trained. The rider can learn to correct the reaction once the rider is knowledgeable and confident of what the reaction will be.

## One Person Stimulus Training

---

**Warning**

One person intense stimulus training while mounted is dangerous, can lead to injury and should be avoided.

---

For years, horse trainers have been "flagging" horses as a means to desensitize them. This is a good beginning exercise, usually done with piece of material on the end of a long whip. It is highly beneficial for the young horse and exposes the youngster to the touch, feel and noise of the material. The average non-professional trainer can build on this technique if it is done while unmounted.

Some of the more common things that an unmounted person can do after following earlier steps in the HSTS™ involve "sacking out" the unsaddled horse.

On Day One of a sacking out process, take a bright-colored towel or gunnysack with you to the stables. While holding the horse in hand in an arena or round pen, let it get a good look at that towel or sack before touching the horse with it. The horse should have the opportunity to sniff it and determine that it will not do any harm. Start on the horse's left side and slowly rub the item down its neck until it is accepted. Rub the front shoulder with the towel, then drape it over the back and rump. If the horse is accepting of this, rub the item around its barrel. When the horse is very comfortable, drape the towel over its head and cover its face with it. If the horse stands, you have definitely reached a hallmark. Once this has been accomplished, move to the horse's off side and do this entire process again. When you have succeeded with both sides, give your horse a break and call it a day. Again, there is no hurry.

On Day Two, take the towel or gunny sack and place several aluminum cans in it (you may have to tie up the towel). Let your horse have another look, shake the item lightly so it knows you have changed the formula. Begin the exact same process that you did the day before. Go slowly, because the added stimulus may get an unexpected reaction. The chances are he will accept this new level of stimulation, especially if you were thorough the day before. If the horse is not accepting, remove the cans and repeat the previous day's lesson with just the towel or bag. Ultimately, the hallmark for this maneuver is to be able to run the "noisy bag" over all parts of the horse and not get a reaction.

On Day Three, take your noisy bag and tie a rope to it. While holding your horse in hand, drop the noisy bag near its front feet. Look for the reaction and allow the horse to settle before moving the bag. If your horse is quiet, pull the bag slowly away from its feet. Give the horse time to lower its head and look at and sniff the bag. Continue this process until there is no reaction, then turn up the heat by lightly throwing the bag against the front legs. You can bet your horse will react to the first feel of the bag on its legs. If the horse is intolerant of this, start over again by rubbing the bag on its neck and around its withers. When it settles, go back to gently bumping the front legs with the bag. This process can go on for sometime and, depending on the horse, a hallmark may be reached when it stands for the noisy bag bumping the front legs.

On Day Four, take the noisy bag and remind the horse that it will not be hurt. Rub it around the back, thighs and rump, being careful of an adverse reaction such as a kick. If the horse is settled, hold the lead rope and swing the bag against the inside of the back legs. Your horse will no doubt react to this by trying to move away or perhaps kick at the item. Be careful of such a reaction. Give the horse time to settle. If the reaction is manageable, complete the process. If it is not, then rub the horse around the back, thighs and rump with the cans until it settles. The hallmark is to be able to bounce the bag off of the back legs without a reaction. Be sure to do this on both the left and right rear sides of the horse, and keep well out of kicking range.

On the last day of bag training take the noisy bag and reintroduce it to the horse. Then swing it around its body and throw it onto its back and rump. Be alert to the reaction. Temper the movements of the noisy bag with the horse's acceptance level. The hallmark for this day is to be able to aggressively swing the bag around the horse and throw it onto any portion of its body without getting a significant reaction.

While a bag or towel tied up with several aluminum cans is not heavy, be mindful not to throw the item with so much velocity as to injure the horse. And of course, stay away from the eyes and face and genitals when doing this.

You can use a number of other items to desensitize the horse to common objects. This is really only limited by your imagination and the realization that you cannot use any item that is going to cause harm. If you mistakenly injure a horse during this process, then you are starting again at ground zero – or perhaps somewhere below that mark. Items that you may find useful include stuffed animals, plastic blow up toys, small rubber balls, plastic bottles filled with pebbles and plastic tarps. No matter what the item, the system is the same: slowly introduce the item, touch the horse on the neck, allow acceptance; gently rub the horse's neck, allow acceptance; rub its front shoulder, allow acceptance; move to the back, thigh and rump, allow acceptance; go around the barrel, allow acceptance; move to the other side and repeat the process.

It is also possible to do one-person desensitization of ground objects on a limited basis. This entails encouraging the horse to step over poles and perhaps onto a wooden bridge. When doing this type of training never stand in front of a horse and attempt to pull him toward you.

When stepping over poles, start with one pole on the ground and begin lungeing your horse on a relatively short line or in a round pen. After the horse is lungeing for you nicely on a line, put the pole on the ground in the track the horse has created. Move the horse off and assist it in getting over the pole by clucking just as the horse gets to it. Most horses will easily walk or trot the pole. Continue this at the walk and trot in both directions. When the horse is very good at this, encourage it to lope the single pole. When your horse easily does all gaits over the pole, then you have reached a hallmark.

Working the horse at a walk over the poles.
They are set 24 inches apart for the walk.

The next thing to do is add additional poles. Place two additional poles on the ground with each pole being approximately 24 inches apart. Work the horse over the poles until it is able to walk them without touching the wood with its hooves. When it has accomplished this, move the poles to 36 inches apart and perform the same maneuver in both directions at the trot. When the horse trots the poles without making contact, you have reached a hallmark and should give that reliable horse the rest of the day off!

Once you have accomplished the ground pole hallmark, place the single pole on a short stanchion (so the lunge line will clear) that is about six inches off the ground. Work the horse over this, gradually raising the height to about 10 to 12 inches. Work at a walk and trot, then add two additional poles, 24 inches apart for the walk (36 inches for the trot) and back to six inches high. Encourage the horse to step over and not gather for a leap. This will help transition to the next exercise, which is the bridge.

Because your horse has successfully traversed a low jump, it is much more likely to go over a step-up wooden bridge. By placing the bridge in the worn track the horse has created on the lunge line or in the round pen, it is difficult to avoid the bridge. However, it may take some encouragement to get it to trust the bridge. Help by ensuring your body position is correct so the horse does not feel that it can retreat through you. If it is tracking to the left, hold the lunge line in your right hand and throw out your left hand if it refuses the bridge and is balking toward you. If the horse attempts to balk away from you, thus avoiding the bridge on the outside of the circle, you need to correct it with the lunge line. If the horse is in a round pen, and you placed the bridge correctly, the wall of the round pen will prevent him from going around to the outside.

It can also be helpful to place the bridge crossways in the horse's path so it does not have to traverse the length of the bridge. If your horse elects to jump the bridge, that is acceptable. Just bring the horse around again at a slow walk and, if it appears to be attempting another jump, correct by pulling slightly on the lunge line and saying, "walk." For some horses, this may take many tries. With perseverance and patience, the horse will eventually walk over the bridge. When it does walk over that scary bridge, reward the horse with an "atta-boy," and a pat. If it has taken some time to accomplish this and because horses learn best through repetition, you may consider one or two more bridge crossings before putting the horse away for a rest.

Needless to say, this system can be used to get a horse to walk over other items such as pieces of plywood, canvas or even plastic tarps. It is a matter of continuing to encourage the horse at the right moment, correcting the miss-steps and rewarding the successes.

## Group Stimulus Training

The best way to do stimulus training is in a group of at least five riders and some ground support personnel. There are a number of reasons for this. The most important is horses like lots of pals around, especially when faced with the stressful nature of stimulus training. In a group of five horses, unless they are all very young, you will almost always find at least one horse that will excel at the training. When the other, more timid, animals see a horse that is willing to try the obstacles, they will often follow suit. This can be a great advantage and can mean the difference between success and failure for the whole group. Conversely, five very young or extremely high-strung horses are only going to reinforce the negative for each other and make the training impossible to accomplish. Balance needs to be reached in the personality and psychological makeup of the animals.

Stimulus training is best done under the supervision of someone who has a great deal of expertise in this area. Unfortunately, there are a limited number of people who are good at this, most of them being either active or retired law enforcement officers. When considering group stimulus training, it is worth the hunt to find a qualified trainer to assist with the process.

A person experienced in the stimulus training of horses must have a fundamental understanding of the process. They must be able to relay these understandings to the riders and ground support personnel. The fundamental understandings are:

· Stimulus training must be done without injury to the rider

· Stimulus training must be done without injury to the horse

· Stimulus training requires that the horse be allowed to win

· Stimulus training requires that the riders stay within the limits of their riding skills

· Stimulus training requires that the riders stay within the limits of their horses' tolerance levels for the training

· Stimulus training is fun and a great educational process

Ground support personnel are absolutely essential in this mix. Persons in this role should be experienced horse people who have a good understanding of the system that is going to be employed. They must know "when to say when" and understand signals that each individual horse may be displaying during the training. They must also be able to encourage the riders, but help to ensure that the riders are not over-riding their abilities or those of their mounts.

Stimulus training is best set up as a course in which each horse has to approach an obstacle and make some accomplishment before riding to the next location. As an example, upon entering the arena, a rider moves to a person holding a large stuffed animal. If the horse is willing to face the person with the animal and take a few steps towards that person, then that may be all that can be accomplished on the first-go-around. The horse then moves on to the next problem where a similar process occurs.

There are ways to make this process easier. The first obstacle that any horse faces upon entering the arena should be low-key. You want the animal to be successful. Obstacles should get progressively more difficult, except the last item. Like the idea that the first obstacle should be approachable, the last should also be easily accomplished. You want the horse and rider to leave the arena with a feeling of success, even if it means they were only able to get through the final challenge. The confidence built by both horse and rider prior to leaving the arena cannot be overestimated and is a critical factor when the teams re-enter the arena to challenge the course a second or third time.

The ground assist person at the first location should have a clear understanding of the importance of allowing the horse to win. One way to ensure this happens is for this person to introduce the obstacle and then retreat from the horse as the animal moves forward. While the horse may be fearful of the item, he obtains a feeling of power as it watches the item give ground as it moves forward. This is a great confidence builder for both horse and rider, which is critical at this juncture of the training.

The obstacles should become more challenging as the rider moves through the course. More challenging can mean more difficult problems, such as walking over a bed mattress, or just turning up the heat by the ground person stationed at the obstacle. As an example, for a very quiet and willing horse, aggressively shaking a bag of cans in its face may not present any stress. However, the next horse in line may not be able to tolerate any noise coming from that bag. The ground person must be sensitive to the differences in each individual's tolerance level.

Horses must be rewarded when they are successful, no matter how slight that success may be. Praise and pets from both the rider and the person on the ground reward the horse that has no fear of the noisy bag. The rider, but not the ground person, rewards the horse that is fearful of the bag, but takes a few steps forward. At this point it is more advantageous to the animal's training that the ground person not drop the bag and approach the horse.

A typical stimulus-training course should have five or six stations to which the horses ride. This is easily done in a 100-foot by 200-foot arena. However, do not try to cram in too many sensory items in too small an area. If sensory items are placed too close together, the horses are unable to deal with one item at a time. It is also advisable to set up a "safe zone" for the horses to take a break. This area should be in the arena and well away from the stimulus-training course. Setting up a safe zone within the confines of the ring means that horse and riders do not have to constantly exit and re-enter the arena. If there is insufficient room within the ring, then the rest area should be outside of the arena.

Once the first horse has been through the course, they should take a short break while the rest of the horses challenge the course. Once the last horse finishes the course, the first horse repeats the course. This allows the animals an additional exposure with plenty of break time for each team, which is crucial to the process. Horses learn through successful repetition. On the second go around, most horses will have a higher degree of confidence and will offer more effort to complete the obstacle. Ground persons will make the course more challenging as the horse and rider teams build confidence. This process is continued until it is obvious that the horses have advanced as far as they are able in the time period allotted for training.

Remember your safety considerations during the training. There is one person responsible for safety. He or she carries the whistle to stop the action. Do not allow horses to bunch up at an obstacle. This will happen if one horse is balking and others are waiting in line. Keep them well separated because the stress of sensory training may cause a horse that is not otherwise known as a kicker to kick.

The one time you may allow horses in very close proximity to each other is when you are using a "mother horse" to assist another in accomplishing an obstacle. A mother horse is one that is willing to accomplish a problem by being ridden next to or in front of an unwilling animal. Often, when the mother horse completes the obstacle, the recalcitrant animal will follow suit. A mother horse must be a non-kicker in all situations, be very tolerant of the other horse and be absolutely steady in the obstacle being attempted. The person riding a mother horse must also be very confident and extra alert to the gyrations of both animals in order to avoid potential injury.

Using a "mother horse" – Senior Deputy Janice Morrill (left) and Dancer guide Citizen Academy Participant Ann Carnathan and her mount Shatzi through the "car wash." Often a calm horse will help a flighty animal get through a tough obstacle.

By permission of Janice Morrill and Ann Carnathan.

## Stimulus Course Levels

There are different levels of stimulus training courses and one should always begin with the least challenging course. A typical beginner course may look something like this:

- **Station 1** – A person with a white towel who attempts to touch the horse on the neck or sides.

- **Station 2** – A person with a plastic or stuffed toy who introduces the item and perhaps touches the horse with it.

- **Station 3** – A white plastic 55-gallon barrel with a stick on it. The rider must approach the barrel, reach down and pick up the stick and strike the barrel, then replace the stick on the barrel. The horse should side-pass to the barrel and stand quietly while the barrel is struck.

- **Station 4** – The noisy bag. The ground person shakes the bag at the horse as he approaches. The horse should continue to move forward toward the bag.

- **Station 5** – A bouncing ball. The ground person bounces the ball around the horse, retreating as necessary to ensure the horse approaches the obstacle.

- **Station 6** – A line of white poles on the ground that the horse is expected to successfully negotiate. This may include side-passing over the poles, backing through an L or other common ground placements.

The next level of a stimulus-training course is an intermediate course. It should only be attempted after successful completion of the beginner's level course. A typical intermediate course may include:

- **Station 1** – A person with the noisy bag or a five gallon plastic bottle partially filled with pebbles or rocks. The expectation is the horse and rider will advance toward the noisemaker.

· **Station 2** – A noisy drag that can be made up of a gunny sack filled with cans or a bag with empty plastic milk bottles inside. The horse must be willing to drag the object a set distance at the walk.

· **Station 3** – A person with pom poms, which are shaken at the horse or handed to the rider. The horse should stand quietly while the rider accepts the pom poms.

· **Station 4** – A line of road flares placed at a great enough interval that riders can snake in and out of the flares without risking stepping on one.

· **Station 5** – The bouncing ball again – but this time the ball is bounced off the horse and the rider must play catch with the ground person.

· **Station 6** – A wooden bridge or sheet of plywood that the horse has to quietly traverse.

And finally for the advanced course:

· **Station 1** – A plastic tarp on the ground (brown is easier than bright blue) folded in quarters. The horse must walk over it.

· **Station 2** – A ground person with smoke producing devices such as smoke candles or grenades or a smoke-producing machine. Horses must learn to tolerate the smoke without shying

· **Station 3** – A square made up of ground poles filled with empty plastic bottles. Horses must walk quietly through the square.

· **Station 4** – The Gauntlet. This is an aisleway consisting of a number of sensory items within it. Items can include mattresses on the ground, balloons, ribbons, tapes, persons with umbrellas, noisemakers, plastic bottles on the ground, etc. The expectation is that the horse and rider will quietly walk through the gauntlet with a minimum of shying and jigging. When doing the gauntlet, be sure to provide an escape route for the horse if it refuses to traverse the obstacle.

· **Station 5** – Perhaps the most challenging obstacle of all is a water crossing consisting of a blue tarp covering a hole in the ground filled with water. For added stimulus, float some shiny pie plates in the water. Then walk the horse through.

· **Station 6** – A ground person with a large ball. The horse must be willing to push or kick the ball with his shoulder or front foot (depending on the size of the ball).

"You've got to be kidding!" you exclaim after reading this list. "My horse will never do all of that!" Well, quite frankly, you are probably right unless you have followed the Horse Sensory Training System™ outlined in this book. In order to be successful, you must:

· Be diligent in your training

· Insure that your horse succeeds at each level before going on

· Proceed slowly and with patience

· Impart bravery to your horse

You can be rewarded with an excellent performance from your equine partner. These are not unusual requirements for police horses. If they can do it, why can't your horse?

Once you have accomplished all or parts of these very difficult obstacle courses, the trick is to reintroduce your horse to the training upon occasion. How often depends on each individual's ability to do the training based on a variety of circumstances. If you can retrain even once a year, you will be surprised at how much improvement your horse will experience. Remember the Key Understanding: the horse never forgets. If he has been successful, not gotten hurt and has a positive experience with the training, then your mount will be prepared to give it another try at a later date. No matter how long it has been, the horse will remember to build on the last positive experience, especially if the retraining is conducted in the same physical location.

Once a year gather up five of your horse friends who have an interest in riding safer horses and put together a stimulus course. Four of the friends can man the obstacles while the first horse and rider go through the course. After the first rider has been successful, that person dismounts and the second person mounts up and challenges the course. By the end of the day, all of the riders should have had an opportunity to accomplish the course.

However, when doing this, remember that the stimulus course is just one component of the Horse

Sensory Training System™ and your ultimate success will depend on how diligent you have been in doing the other components of the system. If you have not ridden your horse in a month or have not worked on connecting through groundwork, then your chances of success in the stimulus course are going to be limited. In other words, to truly sensory train your horse, all components of the system need to be instilled and periodically reinforced in the horse's mind. Only then will you truly be riding a "bombproof" horse.

# Seventh Lesson Learned

I am constantly reminded and amazed at the equine's ability to accomplish a wide variety of tasks when properly trained. This was driven home to me while assisting the Secret Service during the 1996 Presidential Campaign. Our mission was to ride alongside the railroad tracks to escort Vice Presidential Candidate Jack Kemp who was scheduled to do a whistle stop speech aboard a train at a park in a small Southern California town. We were told that there were no anticipated protestors and this detail would be a "piece of cake." Well, that certainly was not how it went.

About 10 minutes before the train arrived, 500 protestors showed up and began to block the railroad tracks. I ordered in the mounted deputies, who were still escorting the train. They arrived after about a mile gallop and began pushing the crowd away from the tracks. They were successful in doing so, which was a good thing, because the train soon arrived traveling at a considerable clip, with banners flying and whistle blaring.

The mounted officers were stationed between the tracks and the crowd, with but a few feet separation. As the situation unfolded, there was a moment when even the crowd got quiet as they looked over this potential wreck. The train flew past, striking one of the horses in the face with a red, white and blue banner. To the amazement of everyone, myself included, absolutely nothing happened. The horses stood their ground, the crowd began to breathe again and the train managed to get stopped at the park. The lesson learned, you ask? Well-trained horses will rise to the occasion and surprise even the most experienced rider in a variety of situations.